Listening to the World

Listening to the World

Cultural Issues
in Academic Writing

Helen Fox
The University of Michigan

National Council of Teachers of English
1111 W. Kenyon Road, Urbana, Illinois 61801-1096

This book is dedicated to the students at the Center for International Education, 1986–1991, who taught me how to listen to the world.

NCTE College Level Editorial Board: Rafael Castillo, Gail E. Hawisher, Joyce Kinkead, Charles Moran, Louise Wetherbee Phelps, Charles Suhor, chair *ex officio*, Michael Spooner, *ex officio*

Staff Editors: Sheila A. Ryan and David Hamburg

Cover Design: Barbara Yale-Read

Interior Design: Tom Kovacs for TGK Design

NCTE Stock Number 29536-3050

Library of Congress Cataloging-in-Publication Data

Fox, Helen
    Listening to the world : cultural issues in academic writing / Helen Fox.
        p. cm.
    Includes bibliographical references and index.
    ISBN 0-8141-2953-6
    1. English language—Rhetoric—Study and teaching—United States. 2. English language—Study and teaching—Foreign speakers. 3. Communication, Intercultural. 4. Multicultural education. 5. Language and culture. I. National Council of Teachers of English. II. Title.
PE1405.U6F69 1994
808'.042'071173—dc20   94-16113
                                                                          CIP

Contents

Acknowledgments

Thanks, first of all, to the faculty at the English Composition Board, University of Michigan, whose devotion to their own scholarly activities, broad intellectual interests, and skeptical, yet friendly reception of my initial ideas gave me an understanding of my audience as well as the courage to begin the writing.

To my students, friends, and colleagues from around the world who told me of their painful experiences writing for the U.S. university and trusted me to make my own meaning of their reflections on communication, teaching and learning, politics, language, and cultural differences.

To all who read my manuscript in whole or in part, asked me tough questions, sent me in new directions, gave me outstanding suggestions and editorial comments, or who simply listened: Kanthie Athukorala, Dianna Campbell, Francelia Clark, Robin Dizard, Peter Elbow, Maria Fox, Nondini Jones Fox, Christina Gibbons, Susanmarie Harrington, Anne Herrington, Emily Jessup, Sara Jonsberg, David Kinsey, Phyllis Lassner, Ilona Leki, Li Xiao Li, Mark Lynd, Marjorie Lynn, Kumiko Magome, Mary Minnock, Hassan Ali Mohammed, Barbra Morris, Anne Mullin, Sharon Quiroz, Marla Solomon, John Swales, Sylvia Tesh, Nick Tsoulos, George Urch, and Robin Varnum.

To my editor and old friend, Dave Stanley, whose work added sensitivity and accuracy to my manuscript, whose kind voice made me willing to read his editorial suggestions again and again.

To Anna Donovan, secretary at the Center for International Education, University of Massachusetts at Amherst, for providing me with an office, a computer, keys to everywhere, and her own upbeat company in the summer of 1992.

To my youngest daughter, Cybelle Fox, who gracefully survived her adolescence despite my obsession with cultural influences on student writing.

And special thanks to my NCTE editor, Michael Spooner, whose gentle support for my decision to write this book for the academy in my own voice despite the risks has been particularly important to me.

Introduction

It is not so much the content of what one says
as the way in which one says it
However important the thing you say
what's the good of it if not heard
or being heard
not felt?

—Sylvia Ashton-Warner, *Teacher*

It is Martin Luther King Day at the University of Michigan, and Alhaji Papa Susso, praise singer and living library of West African family history from the thirteenth century to the present, is visiting the classroom. After playing the *kora*, a twenty-one-stringed harp-lute, for an appreciative audience of upperclass and graduate students, Papa Susso asks for questions. "I'm ready for you," he encourages them, smiling. "I don't feel shy." Talking about his music to foreign audiences is not new for him; Papa Susso has already spoken to American classes on ninety-four campuses in response to the overwhelming new interest in African historical narrative.

For the next hour, students and faculty ask questions, and Papa Susso engages them with stories, humor, and musical interludes. But after he leaves, students are perplexed. Some of them are even angry. "Why didn't he answer our questions?" they wonder. The instructor, whose specialty is oral narrative, is as baffled as the students. "I asked him what he tells his child, who he is raising to be an epic singer, about the qualities that make a great *griot*," the instructor told me. "And he answered totally off the point. He didn't talk about qualities at all. He said, 'you start with the playing,' and then he gave us a list of some typical songs, one after the other. And then he told us how they take a child who is learning to sing from house to house, from king to king. It just didn't make sense. And it wasn't that he didn't understand us. His English is excellent!"

Multiculturalism in the university has come a long way since the 1960s and 1970s, when visits like this one were rare, and classes on oral narrative performance were nonexistent. Since then, many universities have set—and reached—ambitious goals for diversity that have made their student bodies and academic offerings more representative of the world's cultures. But despite these admirable changes, multiculturalism in the university has been limited for the most part to theoretical understanding, a mastery of facts and theories and major ideas, *knowledge about* difference rather than a real *feeling for* what it is to make sense of the world and communicate it in totally different ways. It is this lack of understanding that caused the puzzling miscommunication between Papa Susso and his U.S. audience, and that causes far more serious problems for students from so many of the world's cultures that the university increasingly dedicates itself to serve.

As I viewed and transcribed the videotape made of Papa Susso's visit, I could see why the students were confused. Instead of answering questions directly, Papa Susso showed his respect for the audience by leaving out information that intelligent listeners could infer from the context—that is, what they *might* have been able to infer if they were used to listening to this kind of subtle, understated, conversational style. Instead of speaking in general or abstract terms, he often spoke about the activities that people engage in, leaving it up to the audience to do their own analyses, draw their own conclusions. When students asked him what he thought of Youssou N'Dour, a younger performer who blends ancient rhythms and instruments and singing styles with modern African popular music, Papa Susso skirted the evaluative, analytical question, "What do you think of . . . ?" and answered in concrete terms, indirectly and subtly letting students know that what N'Dour does cannot really be compared with true traditional music— implying but not directly stating a sense of mild disapproval:

> *Q:* What do you think of Youssou N'Dour?
>
> *A:* First of all, he is not a *griot*. He is from the Wolof family. There is a *griot* to the Wolof family; he plays a four-stringed instrument. Youssou N'Dour plays some of the traditional things and some other things. We call what he does "jazz."

Sometimes, instead of answering a question in words, Papa Susso would demonstrate, taking the hand of a fellow performer and showing the audience how he would lead a child "from house to house, from king to king." And instead of prefacing a demonstration with a general statement such as "Our children learn by doing, rather than by listening to advice about qualities," he simply motioned to his colleague, who sat down cross-legged on the floor in order to show—without saying he was showing—how a child learns by sitting at the feet of the master and listening quietly, absorbing the music. Throughout the question and answer session Papa Susso engaged the audience in clapping and singing, in stories and humor, in order to create feelings of group solidarity and congeniality—things he considers essential to good communication. And though the students responded to this and enjoyed it while it was happening, none of these songs, stories, jokes, or demonstrations were connected, in any way they could see, with the simple, direct questions they had asked.

> *Q:* What kind of American music do you listen to, and if you don't, why don't you?
>
> *A:* First of all, I love my music. That doesn't mean your music is wrong. But I love my music. American music is like . . . (high-pitched voice of amazement) Michael Jackson! Because two years ago I was a lecturer in ethnomusicology at the University of California at Santa Barbara, which is not too far from where Michael Jackson is. When he saw on the program somewhere that I was here, he was interested in my music. So I went to his house, and I played for him. And he gave me a check for a lot of money! So I like his music!

Students were frustrated by this kind of evasive response to what they considered perfectly reasonable questions, for here was a cultural resource that they might never be able to tap again. And so they asked their questions in a straightforward, to-the-point way, expecting to hear direct answers that might help them in their scholarly pursuits: tracing the links between African and African American music, for example, or understanding what it is to be a *griot* in modern Africa. And even if they did not have such a serious purpose in mind, asking a friendly visitor to comment on local popular culture would seem quite natural to them from a purely social point of view.

But from Papa Susso's cultural perspective, the "non-answers" that had so confused his audience were completely logical and reasonable. He had worked hard to create an atmosphere where students could absorb knowledge from the entire experience—the music, the demonstrations, the congeniality between performers and listeners. From his point of view, if he were now to engage in direct critique of the culture of his audience, a culture so much a part of *them, their* group, *their* way of expressing themselves, the social harmony that had been created throughout the afternoon might be threatened or even destroyed. Then too, making the kind of concise, evaluative statements the audience expected would involve making his own wordless thoughts and feelings explicit, capturing them in prioritized lists and literal meanings and specific, logical reasons. And as soon as you give reasons, you commit yourself to a particular interpretation of your experience, which somehow devalues all other possible interpretations and obliterates the complex shades of meaning that can reside quite comfortably in the unstated point of a Michael Jackson story. A simple, direct answer would lose all this vital complexity, falsifying the situation, in a way. *What kind of American music do you listen to, and if you don't, why don't you?* This is the kind of question that could take a lifetime to answer!

Neither Papa Susso nor his audience, I would venture to say, was fully aware that their communication styles were radically different, nor were they aware of the values and logical assumptions that lie behind each other's way of understanding the world. But this is not because these styles are so totally foreign to each other. After all, U.S. students know what it is to be subtle, to drop hints rather than to speak directly about a sensitive subject. They know how to tell stories to make a point, and how effective a demonstration can be. And they know what it is to sit passively and learn from a master, or at least to take notes from a university professor.

In the same way, Papa Susso is not incapable of answering directly or analytically. Although he has a tendency to let his audience create their own meanings from the information he presents to them rather than serving it up in neat categories, when it suits his purposes he does answer with the kind of direct, concise information they expect:

> Q: Are *griots* the center of the musical world in Africa?
>
> A: *Griots* are considered the lowest class, but at the same time also considered kings. They beg for a living, therefore they are the lowest, but when it comes to tradition, they are the King.

Though Papa Susso values traditional melodies over popular music and the repetition of ancient wisdom over creative problem solving, one could not say he was therefore unable to figure out how to respond to new situations. If he had to learn everything from ancient wisdom, he would never have found his way around New York City, where he maintains a residence—or for that matter, in his home city of Banjul, The Gambia. And although his concept of himself as an individual is strikingly different from those of the students in his audience, he still holds strong personal opinions, and was concerned enough about his own future employment possibilities to jump up on stage at the Martin Luther King Day ceremony, singing praises to Alex Haley when the author arrived to give the closing address, frightening the wits out of the university security guards and making an indelible impression on his potential new patron. The cultural differences between Papa Susso and his U.S. mainstream audience are tendencies, sometimes strong tendencies, to use particular abilities among many in the human repertoire, to value them, to find them logical, elegant, and sophisticated, to devote considerable attention and care to using them well.

Today, an increasing number of students on U.S. campuses come from cultures that value styles of teaching, learning, communicating, and understanding the world that are different in just these ways— ways that are radically different from the ones most U.S. faculty are familiar with. Total "minority" enrollment in U.S. colleges reached an "all time high" of 20.6 percent in the fall of 1991 (*Evangelauf* 1993, A30) and is expected to continue to climb as immigrants, children of immigrants, and traditionally underrepresented U.S. groups demand and achieve access to higher education. And within that one-fifth of our college population are increasing numbers of students who come on student visas, intending to return to their home countries after their educational sojourn in the U.S.—students from Asia, Africa, the Middle East, and Latin America who enrich the multicultural experience of U.S. mainstream students while they contribute needed tuition money to rising university expenses. And although these students may seem very different in their dress, their interests, their previous education, and their present aspirations from a traditional performer like Papa Susso, still they come from cultures with strong traditions of communicating indirectly and holistically, learning by absorption, valuing the wisdom of the past, and downplaying the individual in favor of the group.

These differences, learned from early childhood, affect the way students interact with their professors and classmates, their attitudes toward the books they read, and the problems they are called upon to solve. They affect how students give oral presentations, from short critiques of articles they've read to dissertation defenses. They affect how students understand assignments, how they study, and how they comment on their classmates' papers. But most of all, these differences affect the way they write. For writing touches the heart of a student's identity, drawing its voice and strength and meaning from the way the student understands the world.

I began to get interested in the problem of how "non western" students express themselves through writing—and how we as instructors often misunderstand them—when I was a graduate student at the Center for International Education at the University of Massachusetts. I had been asked to design and teach a course for graduate students from Asia, Latin America, and Africa by professors who had noticed that these students, who make up half of the Center's student body, often had difficulty with "analytical writing." At first, the precise nature of this difficulty was hard to determine (except, as some faculty members told me, they seemed to write more "description" than "analysis"), but later, after working with the students over a five-year period as colleague, friend, teacher, participant-observer, and researcher; after formal interviews and informal conversations with the students and their professors; after working with individual students, sometimes over a period of years, on their graduate-level writing as editor, coach, teacher, and friend; and after searching the literature, mostly fruitlessly, for help in understanding why these intelligent, highly educated graduate students, most of them mid-career professionals, were having so much trouble with U.S. academic writing, I became convinced that it was because they had a completely different idea of how to understand the world and express that understanding than I did—or than their professors expected. The problem was enormously confusing at first, because many of their difficulties seemed identical to those of immature or inexperienced writers in the western academic context: lack of attention to audience needs, inadequate support, vagueness or sweeping generalizations, trouble making the main point clear, lack of transitions between ideas.

But two things pointed to an important difference between these students and U.S. "mainstream" students I worked with. First, the international students seemed oddly impervious to the repeated and careful explanations by their professors on how to improve their writing, despite the fact that many of these faculty members had worked extensively overseas and had been thesis advisers to graduate students from "non western" backgrounds for fifteen or more years. And secondly, the extent of these difficulties seemed exaggerated, given their level of preparation and their professional status at home. These students had made their way through demanding educational programs in their own countries and were successful as administrators, political activists, development workers, and teachers. Many of them were published writers in their own countries, sometimes even in English. It didn't seem logical that students who had been so successful would write as poorly as some of these students did—so poorly, in fact, that at least one faculty member I interviewed had come to the conclusion that they weren't able to "think" at all. In his view, if you can think clearly, you can write clearly, and what you think will be evident in how you speak about a topic. But these students hadn't had much opportunity to speak up, he had noticed, either in their families or in their education systems, which emphasize rote learning and imitation.

Since curiosity and self-expression had been stifled, students' ability to "think" was limited, and thus any kind of writing that called for analysis or "critical thinking" was bound to be deficient.

But these graduate students—as I knew them as friends and colleagues—were far from un-thinking or un-curious. Informal discussions and out-of-class conversations had long ago revealed the obvious: these students were as talented, observant, and critical—sometimes bitingly so—as anyone in the department. So when I designed my first writing course for these students, I worked on the assumption that complex and original analysis is difficult for anyone returning to school after some years in the work force, and that they probably had little experience writing lengthy papers in their second—or in some cases third, fourth, or fifth—languages. The assignments started with a description or personal narrative and led students deeper and deeper into "analysis" through a "compare and contrast" paper, a "Why does this social or educational problem happen?" paper, and finally a "Why and what to do about it" paper (for example, "Why are there homeless in the U.S.?—Your own analysis and recommendations").

My assumption was that these students, smart and determined as they were, would catch on quickly. But as I taught the course four times over a period of three years and worked with many students individually on their course papers, master's theses, and doctoral dissertations, I continued to find them resistant to my advice to "get to the point sooner" or "reorganize this to make it more clear." Time and time again, some of the students would come back with attempts at reorganization that, from my perspective, were just as disjointed as they had been before. When I compared this process with what happened when I worked with U.S. mainstream students, I realized something was different. The U.S. students who had trouble with analytical papers could not write clearly and cogently, it is true, but they did seem to understand the *idea* behind my advice. "Go into this a little more, tell me why it is true" or "You're a little off the subject here" would usually result in attempts to change the text in the direction I was pointing.

It slowly began to dawn on me that I was assuming that these "non western" students understood the ideas of "organization," "coherence," "clarity," "depth," and "continuity" in the same way I did, when in fact it might not be the case at all. This to me was a clue that cultural differences were involved. I knew I needed to find out from students themselves what kinds of problems they were having and if they could confirm my hunch, by then quite strong, that cultural communication styles learned from childhood were affecting their writing. But getting students to speak frankly with me about the deeply personal issues of writing and culture was not easy. My original research question—"What kinds of difficulties do international graduate students, especially those from developing countries, have with analytical writing?"—had provoked an unexpectedly emotional response from many I posed it to: U.S. professors (all of whom, as it happened, were white males), graduate students from U.S. "mainstream" and "minority" backgrounds, and some of the "non western" graduate students themselves. The professors, sensitive to the possibility they would be perceived as racist, were reluctant to discuss problems of students from ethnic backgrounds that have been historically disparaged by the powerful mainstream European American majority. Mainstream students at the Center were quick to defend their friends and colleagues from the emotional pain that might be caused by such disparaging assumptions. And some of the international students themselves, because of their experience with colonialism and racism, were deeply suspicious of anyone whose questioning might bring the whole issue into the open, especially in a department where they had felt relatively safe, welcomed, included, and inspired by the Center's shared values of empowerment and commitment to social justice.

At first, I found this resistance to my "objective" research question hard to understand. But after many frank conversations and a good deal of reflection, I realized that I might feel similar irritation if someone in my department had thought to investigate the problems that older women returning to graduate school have in trying to write analytical papers, especially if the investigator was a young, self-confident male, who, I might suspect, had doubts about the intellectual abilities of these underprepared women. Regardless of this hypothetical male's protestations of objectivity (so much like my own), regardless of his "altruistic" motives of helping people like me, would I really be able to look him in the eye with respect? Who had asked him for help, anyway? Perhaps, I mused, I too would begin to feel like an unwilling subject whose real or imagined weaknesses would be exposed by such an academic investigation, backed by the status of the researcher himself and, behind him, by the authority of the university.

Imagining myself in such a situation helped me understand how my interest in this topic must have appeared to both international students and their defenders at the Center. But because I was a participant-observer with a long-term agenda, I had already begun working on the necessary relationships that would be strengthened and validated over time, eventually allowing a sense of trust to develop around this touchy issue. I tried to be open with everyone, talking at every opportunity about my assumptions and my tentative findings, asking for feedback, objections, and questions at every stage. Sometimes I did this in writing, stuffing the mailboxes of all fifty-six on-campus Center graduate students with summaries of my research to date, my plans for the next step, and my interest in their feedback. Other times I talked with students behind closed doors—in my car, driving a departing international student to the airport; at coffee shops, surrounded and protected by the chatter of students from other colleges; or on my back porch, looking out into the pine forest over a glass of wine. Finally, students began to reveal their long-held frustrations about writing and began to speculate with me about why all this was happening—why the issue was so touchy, so political, and, at the same time, so crucial to their success at the university.

The formal, structured part of my study involved in-depth interviews with seven professors, the four faculty members at the Center and three from other departments who worked extensively with international graduate students. In order to get around their resistance to questions about the problems of this population, I began by asking them to comment on the difficulties that graduate students in general have with writing analytical papers, and then asked them who, in their experience, had such difficulties and why this might be so. By this circuitous route, these faculty members began to identify students from abroad, especially students from "non western" backgrounds, as those with particular difficulties in this area.

I also asked these professors to tell me their definition of "analysis" or "analytical writing" in order to understand more precisely what it was that these students couldn't do very well. This question was surprisingly difficult for them to answer, despite their confidence in using these terms in the language of their assignments ("Present an analysis of your country's educational heritage since 1900 . . . an analysis of basic ideologies and values . . . an analysis of forms and processes of education) and their feedback to students ("This paper could be strengthened with a bit more analysis . . . "). To help them with this task, I asked them to show me concrete examples of "good" and "poor" analysis on students' course papers, master's theses, and doctoral dissertations and to tell me why they judged them the way they did. Examples of "good analysis" could come from either mainstream or "non western" students, while "poor analysis" was to come from "non western" students so that I could pinpoint the difficulties of this particular group.

From these conversations about writing I began to realize that what the professors meant by "difficulties with analysis" went far beyond the "writing problems" that they expected me to help students correct. Good analytical writing, as these faculty members were describing it, involves a multitude of values, skills, habits, and assumptions about audience needs: it means setting down a clear, step-by-step, transparently logical progression of ideas; it means critically examining a variety of ideas and opinions and creating an original interpretation that shows, very explicitly and directly, the writer's point of view. It means using reference materials to add evidence and authority to the writer's own argument, weaving together material from a variety of sources into a pattern that "makes sense" to the reader. It means attributing ideas to individual authors with meticulous care. It means speaking with a voice of authority, making judgments and recommendations and coming to specific, "reasoned" conclusions. It means valuing literal meanings and precise definitions and explicit statements of cause and effect. It means writing sparsely and directly, without embellishments or digressions, beginning each paragraph or section with a general, analytical statement and following it with pertinent examples. In short, it is at once a writing style, a method of investigation, and a world view that has been part of western cultural heritage for hundreds of years and that is learned through a process of both formal and informal socialization that begins in early childhood, especially by those who come from "educated families," go to "good schools," and aspire to positions of influence and power in the dominant culture. But I did not understand all this at the time. It came only gradually to me, as students began to talk to me about their own socialization processes, their cultural assumptions and values, their communication styles, both oral and written, and their difficulties understanding why they didn't seem to catch on to this thing called "analytical writing" as easily as they or their professors had expected.

These insights from students came, as I have indicated, from my informal conversations over the years with friends and colleagues from "non western" backgrounds as well as from formal interviews with sixteen graduate students who were, in most cases, students of mine. They came from twelve countries: Korea, Japan, the People's Republic of China, Indonesia, Nepal, India, Sri Lanka, Côte d'Ivoire, Somalia, Cape Verde, Brazil, and Chile. I kept notes and a teaching journal for the four courses in writing for international graduate students that I taught over a three-year period at the Center, and collected many students' papers, along with notes of how we had worked through some of their writing difficulties, as well as their explanations of what they had been trying to express in their papers, how they had misunderstood assignments, and their ideas about the connections between language, writing, and culture.

The following year, as a newly appointed faculty member at the English Composition Board at the University of Michigan, I continued my observations while working with both graduate and undergraduate students from a variety of cultural backgrounds, including many from the European American majority. Many were my students in an introductory course in academic writing which they were obliged to take if they showed, by a timed essay assessment as they entered the university, that they needed help in formulating and expressing an "academic argument." These classes are small (no more than sixteen students) and intensive (four hours a week plus a half-hour individual conference for each student once a week for seven weeks), so it was possible to get to know the students and their writing quite well. The rest of the students who appear in these pages came to my office for Writing Workshop, a student service consisting of scheduled, private writing conferences for students who are working on papers in a great variety of disciplines, half an hour a week for undergraduates, an hour for graduate students. All in all, I estimate that in that first year, I saw in individual conference more than four hundred students from all across the university, some from abroad, some from the U.S. multicultural population, many from "mainstream" U.S. culture.

The more students talked to me, and the more I learned how to talk with students from different cultures about their writing, the more I became convinced that it is the ways students have learned to see the world, to see social relations and identity and the negotiation of social roles, that affect the way they express themselves, both in speaking and in writing. Though cultural differences in writing styles had been noted in the 1960s by Robert Kaplan (1966; see also 1972, 1982), the paragraph types that he had identified as coming from particular linguistic and cultural systems—Oriental spiral, Semitic parallelism, Romantic digressions (in contrast to the English "straight line" construction)—were only a small part of the puzzle I was seeing. While it is true that some countries, such as Japan and China, do have unique, historically based writing styles (though these styles are not necessarily used for academic writing), the writing styles of former colonies such as Côte d'Ivoire have a more complex history; while their academic style is modeled after that of their colonizers, student writing also seems to be influenced by the rich mixture of African and European languages and cultures that have been part of their lives since childhood. And to add even more complexity, students from countries such as Somalia that have only recently formalized a written version of their national language and who may therefore be unfamiliar with the conventions of written reference and support for argument may be deeply affected by oral styles of expression as well as other influences of their culture.

In addition to the variety of languages and cultures that may affect academic writing, I found that students tend to communicate differently, both orally and in writing, according to their gender, their status at home (both in the larger society and within their own families), the area of the country where they grew up, the degree of their family's "westernization," the amount and types of writing they have done in the past, their fluency in English, and their understanding of U.S. culture, particularly the culture of the university. Personality seems to play a part, too; some students in my study were extremely resistant to adopting U.S. academic style and expressed feelings of anxiety and depression over their sense that they were being asked to abandon their identities, their ways of thinking and self-expression, while others seemed to view the new writing style as a welcome addition to their repertoire of ways to understand the world and express themselves in it.

All these factors of culture, education, gender, status, personality, and willingness to be "obedient to the system," as one student put it, affect the writing of our multicultural student population. It is not enough, anymore, to see the difficulties our students may have in the university as "language problems" or inadequate academic prepared- ness that can be alleviated with remedial work in English or basic skills. Nor is it enough to think of students who come from other cultures as having distinctive, culturally based writing styles which we can either encourage or ask them to change. For although culture has a strong influence on the writing that all students produce, their writing "styles" do not come in neat packages; they are as complex and varied as the personalities and life experiences of each individual in the human family.

As a teacher and researcher who has lived and worked most of my adult life outside my own culture, I have been observing for many years how people communicate—and miscommunicate—across dif- ferences in language, education, class, gender, personality, life expe- riences, upbringing, and basic assumptions about how to make sense of the world. I have come to the conclusion, after thirty years of watching, that many of the tensions between people—both the every- day variety and the violent ones that cause so much trouble in the world—are caused by the difficulties we have in stepping outside ourselves and seeing how the world might make sense from another perspective.

While this is not a new observation, it is, I think, a crucial one. I hope to show in this book that the dominant communication style and world view of the U.S. university, variously known as "academic argument," "analytical writing," "critical thinking," or just plain "good writing," is based on assumptions and habits of mind that are derived from western—or more specifically U.S.—culture, and that this way of thinking and communicating is considered the most sophisticated, intelligent, and efficient by only a tiny fraction of the world's peoples. If faculty want to encourage a deeper, more meaningful multiculturalism, we need to recognize that many of our students have been brought up to think and express themselves very differently, and that these ways are worthy of our attention and understanding.

1 Frustrations

As a writing instructor at a large, elite university, I have the luxury of spending most of my time seeing students one by one. They come to Writing Workshop from all across the disciplines, papers in hand, needing to talk through their ideas, or figure out what their main point is, or how to make their paper flow. I see undergraduates wrestling with the poetic significance of light and dark in the *Aeneid*, or searching for a glimmer of understanding of feminist jurisprudence, or Roman architecture, or Christianity in Africa. I've seen a young prodigy, ready to embark on original doctoral research in biochemistry, paralyzed by writer's block. I see perfectionists, asking if I follow an extended metaphor, or if I can find any commas out of place in a discussion of the construction of gender in speeches by Pakistani politicians. And I see students who don't understand the reading, or who have not yet thought deeply about the topics they were assigned, or whose ideas are so complex they are unable to say anything coherent, either on paper or to me.

Although most of the writers I see these days are from the European American "mainstream," increasing numbers come to this university—and to most U.S. universities—from a variety of cultures around the world. Our students come from ninety-six countries, many as newcomers, others as longtime U.S. residents who seem totally "Americanized," but whose ways of thinking and expressing themselves still show the deep influence of the communication styles of their parents or extended families. The requests of these students are often a little different from those of the mainstream students who have historically filled our university classrooms. These students are seeking help with general "language" problems: grammar, they say, or "proofreading." Some are simply confused by their instructors' feedback, though they have been trying their best to figure it out. Graduate students are often sent by professors who are unable or unwilling to give them much feedback on content because they can't make heads or tails of the argument.

Sometimes their instructors have grown irritated: "Haven't they had English classes?" they ask. "Haven't they been taught about topic

1

sentences, logic, flow, transitions? Surely there are differences in the ways they have learned to write in their own cultures, or in their own languages, but why haven't they learned what good writing is in English?" Other instructors, in the spirit of multiculturalism, have announced to their classes that styles coming from other traditions are welcome. But when it comes to reading the results of their open-minded assignments, they may not understand what they see.[1]

Sarita holds a Ph.D. in musicology from India and speaks five languages. She has been in the U.S. for a good twenty years; her husband is an auto company executive, her children grew up here and are now off in college. "So," she tells me smiling, "I thought I would do something." She has been taking graduate courses in the Asian studies department and is now thinking of switching to library science, but in both departments she's been having trouble with the writing.

The paper she has brought to show me—on copyright law and control and access to information—seems extremely disjointed. She starts historically, somewhere in the Middle Ages, then gives her whole argument in a single paragraph on page one, then goes back and gives what seems like stream-of-consciousness information which has only a faint and fleeting connection with the points she tells me she is trying to make.

Over the course of the next few weeks I see this paper five times, and each time we spend an hour unraveling it, page by page, draft by draft, trying to find a way to package it differently, with a thesis up front and the major points separated into sections, connected by clear transitions. It is slow going, but Sarita is happy she has found me, she says, because I have taught in India, and so I know that it's different there. This seems to be very important to her, to be working with someone who knows it's different. It's not even so important to her that I know *how* it's different; she doesn't ask me what I think of any of the details of Indian life, or thought, or habits of mind. She seems to sense my conviction that the differences in her background are the cause of many of the problems she has in communicating with her readers, and that I find these differences interesting, rather than some sort of deficit.

Sarita had taken an advanced course in dissertation writing for non-native speakers three years ago and, according to her professor, she had done poorly. At that time, her major problem had been lack of production—she couldn't seem to come up with more than half a page on any topic. Her professor knew that she had an extensive background in music, and so, he said, "It wasn't a content problem. Probably it had to do with her having taken so much time off and just not being used to writing now." I wasn't so sure. If writing and thinking are so closely connected, why not just write down the thoughts as they come to you? Surely this was not a problem with thinking in general, or with motivation, or with vocabulary.

I called Kamala, an old friend originally from Sri Lanka, and told her about Sarita—that she was from India, that she spoke five languages, that she had a Ph.D., and that her papers were awfully confused—or maybe it was that *I* was awfully confused, reading them. Kamala was consumed by laughter. "And it probably will take her five years to catch on," she said, gasping for breath. *"It sounds so familiar."*

Kamala had been suffering from writer's block for months when I met her. Although she had spoken English for more than thirty years and had been accepted into a doctoral program at a major U.S. university, writing anything was terribly difficult for her. She would sit at the computer for hours, but the thoughts did not come. She would accumulate "incompletes" in her course work by not handing in final papers. When she did write, her papers would come out confused, overly complex, and in her words, "without meaning, sometimes, without any connection."

Professors would tell Kamala that her writing "needed improvement" and sometimes would patiently show her where she was leaving out important information or where the sentences were too long or seemed tangled, but these comments had the effect of setting her back even more. "I felt like a misfit," she told me, "very unwanted, very put down. I thought everybody must be laughing at me. I wondered if people knew that I had a culture of my own, or that there are even any worthy people in my society. I even wondered what people here must think of Buddhists. Are we a passive group of people? Can't we do anything without being told?"

As Kamala and I became friends, we would meet every Sunday for breakfast and, when the weather was nice, we would sprawl out on the grass on the town common to go over her papers. She would listen intently to my suggestions and make careful corrections, but although she seemed to understand my explanations, her ability to produce papers did not improve; in fact, it seemed that her block was intensifying.

One day, however, she came over to my house to show me something that she'd had no trouble writing at all. "But that's because it's just a story," she told me, intercepting my congratulations, "something to be read aloud." She had been asked to give an oral presentation at a conference and, without any compulsive preliminaries, had sat down and typed a smooth, clear, four pages on women's use of silence as a way to exercise strength and power.

Kamala was convinced that no one could possibly understand the piece unless she read it aloud. Only then would she be able to give it the inflection and the tone that the audience would need in order to *feel* as well as hear her words. "If you gave this to an American and watched their face as they read," she told me, "I'm sure you would see they did not understand some parts. Because they would not hear my intonations and the place where I break, the places where I stress, so they would not know I wanted to stress those things." She picked up her paper and moved to the edge of the couch, sitting up straight as if she were about to sing:

> *My mother would not support me openly, but she did not seem to think I was out of line. In her own way, she would indicate to me that I was OK.* (short pause) *I felt it. That gave me a strength that I could not explain.*

"You see?" Kamala put down her text and smiled at me as if her demonstration made her point obvious. "So I think that if this paper were to be read by a professor," she said, laughing at the thought of it, "he would say, 'I don't quite catch your meaning here. You must give the reader some idea of what your point is!' And I have not done anything like that," she said, her voice trailing off uncertainly. "But I know that this is very effective, as I read it . . ."

Yang Li is an eighteen-year-old from Taiwan who placed out of the freshman requirement in introductory composition, but asked to do an independent study in academic argument with me anyway so that he could be even more prepared, four years later, to get into a U.S. law school. He is a quick thinker with an impressive knowledge of international politics and is awfully good at doing what he was trained to do in Taiwan. As I tell him this, he smiles slightly, remembering. He is not even protesting politely anymore that he is unworthy and that his writing is terrible. Yes, he did have an old life, six months ago, and he was successful at it. But adjustment here has not been so easy. For the last few weeks he has come into my office totally disheveled, out of breath, his whole body an apology.

Today, though, he seems to have come to terms with something. He didn't even flinch when he saw the C I had put on his paper. He had insisted that I give it a grade, even though it was only a draft, so he would know how he was doing. I had given the paper a long, careful look, commenting at each place where he had used emotional language or where he had breezed through the argument with the blithe assurance that everyone would agree with him, or would agree to agree for the sake of solidarity.

I explain again, as I had explained to him so many times, that U.S. academic style demands that you pick a subject apart carefully, bit by bit, that you look at every piece separately and ask why or how— weighing it, judging it. I tell him that if he doesn't do this, if he keeps speaking in generalizations, if he keeps trying to get group consensus through scolding, that he might well be criticized for not thinking deeply enough about his subject or analyzing it with enough care. He looks puzzled when I say this. It is clear to both of us that he has an extraordinarily critical mind.

"You didn't realize what you had signed up for, did you, when you asked me to help you learn U.S. style?" Yang Li is quiet, thoughtful, for a moment. Then his expression stiffens, and he sets his jaw hard.

"Change," he says grimly.

———

Joseph walks into my office, drops his book bag and wearily begins taking off layers of winter clothes, draping them over chairs, sighing softly. I introduce myself and ask him where he's from. "Nigeria," he says, rummaging through the book bag and drawing out a handful of papers. I am delighted, I tell him; I have worked briefly in Togo and Côte d'Ivoire. Joseph looks up at me smiling, curious, almost hopeful. I ask him what I can do for him. "I'm so . . . just . . . so . . . " he says, shaking his head to emphasize his state of mind: fed up, discouraged, disappointed with himself, his instructor, the school, the whole experience.

"Nigeria was colonized by the British," he begins, sighing wearily again, "and so English is spoken widely there."

"I know," I say, smiling.

He nods in my direction. But he has little hope, yet, that I will understand. Because *he* doesn't understand. He has been getting *C-pluses*, *B-minuses* on his freshman English papers, and that just is not acceptable. "No," he shakes his head. "That is totally out of the question. I am accustomed to being an *A* student."

He shows me his instructor's comments on a paper he has titled "The Displacement of My Ping Pong Bat and Myself." The remarks are sincere, well written, kind:

I appreciate your efforts to introduce your own case of displacement with general remarks on the subject. These preliminaries are quite elaborate and long-winded though: they could use quite a bit of editing. I tend to resist or disbelieve some of this, too, such as the bit about most people you know nearly going insane (maybe you know different people than I do!) and the supposed universality of your own situation. . . . Your story is interesting, I think, not because it's typical but because it's exceptional, extreme. . . . C+

I read through his paper and tell him right away that I can see some differences between the way he is expressing himself and what his instructor is expecting. "In the U.S. everything is direct, everything is rapid," I tell him. "You have to get into the subject right away, no preliminaries. People don't see the point of getting to know each other first, of getting into the subject slowly, savoring it." Joseph is looking at me closely.

"And so you see, to the U.S. reader, your story sounds long-winded and should be edited. And then the TA's comment about not believing you? There is no appreciation here of exaggeration for effect. You see, you said that most people you know have almost gone insane dealing with displacement? You've got to realize that you're dealing with a very literal culture here. When you say "most people almost go insane," they really think you mean that most . . . people . . . really . . . almost . . . go . . . insane!"

Joseph rolls his eyes. "Oh my God," he says. "I can't believe it."

Fumi is a Japanese graduate student in Middle Eastern studies. She used to be a water ballet champion and traveled throughout the Pacific Rim as a teacher and judge for international competitions. Personable, erudite, she has recently won a prize for her mastery of spoken Arabic. But after working for an hour with her I am completely exhausted. Her paper is on Islamic law, and its vocabulary is new to me, so I have to keep referring back to the definitions of terms, which, fortunately, she has included in the opening of her paper. But the combination of a Middle Eastern subject, the Japanese manner of thinking and expression, and the attempt at U.S. academic style is too much for my feeble brain. Fumi has been patient with me, though occasionally her voice rises with exasperation at my slowness, my inability to catch her meaning. So the second time she comes in for help with the same paper, I brace myself for another difficult hour.

Yes, again it is the same. Fumi explains her meaning over and over, but I am lost in the fuzzy verbs. Every paragraph seems to begin with "there exists," "there are," or "it has"; weak, passive constructions that leave me wallowing, flailing in molasses.

Here again, there are some quotations used in support of the mufti's opinion . . .

"So what?" I ask myself. I look for a way to say this more politely. I explain the need to use words that emphasize action, rather than a quieter, more contemplative way of existing, like flowers in a garden. Fumi laughs at the flower image, but there is an edge of irritation in it. I talk about the need for transitional markers to help me understand the direction the paper is heading. But it is only later that I notice how many signposts she really had planted in this argument. In fact, nearly every sentence starts with a "moreover," "furthermore," "nevertheless," "also," "despite the fact that," "whereas," or "here again."

Here again, there are some quotations used in support of the mufti's opinion, especially in Ibn Habib's fatwa. Moreover, the intention (niyya) of the words uttered by the accused is the object of the discussion. Whether there is a consideration of the real meaning of the words or not by muftis differs. While Ibn Habib and Sulayman interpreted Harun's words in a good way, Khalid considered that Harun's words should be taken to the letter. This difference in interpretation of the words can be also found in the other articles. Furthermore, as seen in the two fatwas of Ibn Habib and Sulayman, there is a variety in the reasoning process despite the fact that the conclusion is the same. . . .

I glance at the clock. We are about twenty minutes into the hour appointment and I still have not understood the first paragraph. I stifle the urge to laugh, weakly and hysterically, at my own ineptness. We are both leaning over the desk, and I am holding the paper under the strong desk lamp, as if its brightness and heat could illuminate the words. Hysteria grips me again and I bite the inside of my cheek, the way I did as a teenager, sitting with my high school choir in the front row in a synagogue, listening to a cantor who bellowed like a bull, eyeing the other choir members down the line, all biting their lips, the bolder and more self-controlled among them raising one eyebrow. Oh God, I don't want to laugh. This will be entirely misinterpreted. Tears escape from the creases around my eyes. I force myself to concentrate on Fumi's words one at a time. But the Arabic terms, whose meanings I have so soon forgotten, suddenly sound humorous too.

Finally I just move on, searching for something easier to understand. I try to explain the necessity of the "topic sentence" for the western reader, something which Fumi has heard many times before. She is trying hard to see the logic of it; I can tell by the way she listens, seriously, to my explanation. But she is not convinced.

"Japanese is more vague than English," she tells me. "It's supposed to be that way. You don't say what you mean right away. You don't criticize directly." I am struck by the fact that even though she knows that U.S. academic style is different, even though she's heard about the needs of the western reader, she still needs to let me know that her way of thinking makes sense.

"It's supposed to be that way," she repeats, unsmiling, as if I won't believe her.

Carlos leans back in his chair quietly, almost regally, as I review his paper on economic theory. His elegant bearing is reflected in the voice I hear in his paper. Though he arrived from Argentina only last year, his English is nearly flawless; he has few grammar errors, a sophisticated vocabulary. Only a few odd turns of phrase catch my eye, but even these work well here; they add character, originality. But regardless of his command of English, the thread of his argument is hard to follow. He begins clearly enough, almost mechanically, with a thesis that proposes to be reasonable and interesting. But soon this idea trails off and other ideas take its place. Unlike Fumi's paper or Sarita's, his writing doesn't leave me floundering, struggling to understand. I feel more like I'm floating down a river, taking in the ever-changing scenery. I am engrossed in each idea as it passes—but the excursion is nothing like the guided tour that had been announced to me at the beginning of the voyage.

I start to tell Carlos that I've seen such strategies before from writers from Latin America, but he stops me cold. "This has nothing to do with cultural differences," he says. "It's just a problem I have. I have often been told I have a tendency to get off the subject." I don't argue with him, of course, as this seems to be a sore point with him. I do tell him, though, what Latin American students from countries as diverse as Brazil, Puerto Rico, and Chile have told me about both writing and intellectual conversation—the emphasis on the surrounding context rather than on the subject itself, the importance of digressions in saying everything that needs to be said, the tendency of the great Latin American writers to encompass the world rather than to dissect it microscopically.

With this, Carlos agrees. "It's impossible to say everything you have to say all at once," he says, "you have to keep coming back to it. All the ideas are connected." He nods slowly, thinking. "It's true, Latin

American writers do tend to digress. Well, maybe that *is* what I'm doing in my introduction here."

———————

I talk with a tenured faculty member originally from the Middle East about what I have been finding in my study over the past seven years. Working with him on a committee to investigate the quality of life for international students, I have noticed how direct and to the point he is as a meeting chair, how task oriented he is, even for an American. No time for digressions in this committee, no comfortable chatter. "How did you learn to write for the U.S. university?" I ask him. He winces, remembering his graduate student days. "It was beaten into me," he says. "I wrote draft after draft, and they kept telling me it was no good, that I couldn't write. I resisted, but they just beat me harder."

———————

At the end of the term, after exams are over, Writing Workshop becomes a little more relaxed. I turn on my radio and putter around contentedly while students miss their appointments or come in asking me to take a quick look at a cover letter for a summer internship or to make suggestions about their resumé. But one day, a scared-looking sophomore shows up in my office. "I'm here because I didn't do very well in freshman composition," she says, "and I want to understand why." An unusual request, on a beautiful summer day, for a young person to make on her own initiative. "Sandra Chen," her papers say. Her spoken English is completely American, right down to the age-specific slang. She was born here, she tells me, though she and her parents speak Chinese at home. She is an only child, and comes from a town where she never had many friends, never felt comfortable. *"Students in my high school were narrow-minded and ignorant,"* one of her papers says. *"In the hallways I was pushed around by these people who thought they were royalty. I must have appeared to be a peasant in their eyes."*

We look at her instructor's comments carefully; they seem to center around lack of evidence and overgeneralization. In a paper she calls "Jester," Sandra talks about feeling overwhelmed by the number of white students at her large high school:

> *I had this notion that these students would gang up on me, therefore, right from the beginning I had surrendered my dignity to them. In my mind I imagined all the students ridiculing me because I was not the same breed as they were. . . .*

"You've got some terrific, almost poetic writing here," her instructor has remarked in the margin. The word "breed" is circled, with "word choice" written above it.

> Sometimes I would just be minding my own business and of course some of the guys, "the untouchables," had to feel superior by making fun of me. Even though my back may have been facing them I could always feel at least twenty pairs of eyes piercing right through me and their laughter echoing in my mind. Why am I always the center of derision?

"Were they laughing at you, or were you just imagining it? Sounds like the latter," her instructor has written. Sandra is not offended by this remark, only confused. We look at the comments at the end of the paper, next to the B−/C+.

> What's interesting about this essay is the fine line between what you were imagining as abuse and what truly was abusive. At this point it's very hard to tell because there are no specifics. . . . My sense is that this was all a horribly subtle thing, but then you still need to find specific examples of what felt like real abuse and what might have been an overreaction on your part.

I talk with Sandra a little about the importance of subtlety and feeling in East Asian cultures and the need, in the U.S. academic context, for proof and specific examples, even when some subtlety may be recognized. As we talk about how in another cultural context it really is possible to know something with certainty, even when it's happening behind your back, Sandra's frightened face is transformed by a beautiful smile. "I want to come here on a regular basis," she says. "Writing is my weakness. I really want to improve."

———

These students that I see in Writing Workshop are not "minority" students, in world terms. They are the World Majority. And we need to pay attention to them, to learn how the world makes sense to them, both to broaden our own intellectual interests and capabilities and to become more effective at helping them adopt the communicative styles and habits of mind that will foster their success in our system. These students want to learn what the university expects of them; they are accustomed to doing well in their home countries, and they want to continue to excel. But reaching them is not always easy, even when we are well meaning and knowledgeable. Students are resisting, and we react, sometimes, with exasperation, for we may underestimate how difficult it is for them to change not only their writing style, but the way they think about themselves and the world. And because of our country's long history of ethnocentrism and racism, students may be insulted when we bring up the subject of "difference," for which they read "deficiency." We have to tread carefully. But we do have to understand.

2 Worldwide Strategies for Indirection

A professor of political science has devised an ingenious first writing assignment to help his students understand how to put together a term paper. Students are to imagine that they have been wait-listed for his course and to convince him in writing that they should be allowed to enroll in it. The point of the assignment is to help students think out, in an immediate, personal way, how they would naturally structure an argument. "If you had sixty seconds of your instructor's time," he says, "how would you make your most convincing case?" The reason he sees this as a necessary first assignment is that many students, even in their junior year, do not yet see that in its simplest form an academic argument is just a clear, direct thesis ("I should be allowed into this course") followed by convincing reasons that support it, with either explicit or implicit attention paid to possible objections. Students don't need to think very hard to write this paper and can be expected to come up with something like this: "I need to take this course in Third World Politics for a number of reasons. First, I have an interest in going abroad in the future; second, it is a prerequisite for a course in international law which my adviser tells me I should take next semester; and third, a modern liberal education means knowing not only about our own society, but about problems faced by countries less fortunate," etc. etc. As students put together this simple argument, they can easily see that in addition to its "natural" structure, the argument should sound assertive and confident, that it should be short, logical, and to the point, without irrelevant digressions, and that its tone should be polite and reasonable rather than strident or badgering.

All very simple and clear. But in my own class in academic argument, Shu Ying, a new student from Taiwan, has approached me with a similar request: that I allow him to miss the first hour of every class and give him an extra half-hour of one-to-one conference time every week to make up for it. Clearly, this is a proposal for which he needs to make a convincing case. But how does he design his argument? He does not simply tell me his reasons in a straightforward way, polite but assertive, to the point so as not to waste my time. Instead, he silently shows me his schedule, waiting for me to notice that his Chinese class conflicts with the first hour of my course. He does not advance crucial information, but waits until I ask for it—that all other sections of the writing course are closed and that he needs my course this term in order to get into the intellectual meat he has been waiting for, the classes in philosophy and history that he could take in his sophomore year. He does not mention these facts or his own personal wants and needs partly out of deference to my status as his instructor and partly out of simple politeness, which requires that he not insult my intelligence by telling me directly what I could figure out for myself.

Besides these strategies of polite omission, Shu Ying has been doing me schoolboy favors, erasing my blackboard after class, asking my advice about other courses he is taking, working to establish a relationship that would leave me feeling obligated to bend the rules for him. His strategies for arguing his point, effective in his own society—and who knows, maybe effective with me, too—are far from a model for the first assignment in the political science class; they are not the moves that in the U.S. context would "naturally structure" an argument. In fact, what seems natural to Shu Ying is strangely reminiscent of what he has been doing on some of his papers—leaving out some of the obvious, or seemingly obvious, points that he needs to make a convincing case. And this, of course, is the reason he needs to take my class, even though in many respects his English writing skills are superior to those of many of my U.S. "mainstream" students.

While Shu Ying's care not to insult his audience leads him to make omissions that seem odd in the western context, other students from cultures that value subtlety of expression may have the opposite problem: putting in *too much* information—piles of facts or stories or data that seem unconnected to the original assignment and that lack any analysis of what this information might mean. Professors I interviewed for my study would show me excerpts from doctoral theses written by world majority students, telling me how difficult it sometimes was to convince them not to spend time writing material that would just have to be cut later. "What he wrote was the history of, the geography of—it didn't have anything to *do* with what he was trying to get at," said one professor of a Kenyan doctoral student. "I don't mind the history—just so long as it's related to the topic." Another faculty member, who had worked with a Malaysian doctoral candidate "two days out of five for a period of weeks," told me what a trial it had been to get this obviously bright, well-prepared student through the writing of his thesis. "I would find extensive digressions that he hadn't mentioned previously. Or things that he had mentioned previously that he hadn't gone into as he had suggested he would. And then he would go and get excessive amounts of research and present it to the point of overkill. His related research chapter runs something like a hundred pages!" A third professor, who had worked extensively with graduate students and visiting scholars from South Asia, was particularly exasperated by what he called "the list phenomenon." "I see it in senior officials to junior graduate students: just unvarnished lists, a list of this and a list of that. You know, we're going to discuss the philosophy of a literacy program, and so there's a list of twenty items. There's no discussion besides maybe some amplifying description. Uh . . . and then the law was passed and that enabled something, and then fifteen subsections, listed. Stuff which we would consider useless or appendix material is presented as text."

Both of these strategies—subtle, sensitive omission and conscientious attention to context—produce what U.S. faculty members see as a disjointedness that is also characteristic of many of the papers written by U.S. mainstream students: papers from inexperienced writers, papers from fluent writers who aren't yet sure what they want to say, papers from writers who don't know their audience or who haven't realized they're supposed to think about audience, papers from students who suspect they are dyslexic, papers from students who have immersed themselves in their topic for so long they have lost all sense of perspective. But the indirect strategies of world majority students are not the result of inexperience or confusion, but of training and purpose, for they have been brought up to value a subtle or roundabout communication style as polite and sophisticated. They may not be very good at it, of course, just as U.S. mainstream students are not always good at being direct and precise. The elaborate metaphor, the illustrative story without explicit commentary, the comparison without direct contrasts between the things being compared may not be crafted well enough to convey meaning even in a culture with a high tolerance for the contextual or the symbolic. These students may, in fact, just have a *feeling* about the way they want to present themselves, a voice that holds back, or talks around, or strives for a kind of relationship between the reader, the text, and the self that is markedly different from what is expected in the U.S. context.

In addition to this cultural difference, world majority students are subject to all the same sources of difficulty that U.S. mainstream students are: they may have done inadequate research on the topic, or finished their paper at three in the morning, or misunderstood the reading, or the assignment, or both, or, as is quite common, they may have had very little experience writing papers in any language. The stories behind specific features of world majority students' papers can be so complex and varied that it is impossible—in my experience at least—to understand where the difficulties lie by looking at the texts alone. If our aim is to discern anything as elusive as the impact of culture, we also need to become familiar with the individual students— their personalities, their educational backgrounds, their levels of understanding and maturity—and to learn something about the cultures that have informed their assumptions, their expectations, their views of themselves and the world. And when we have begun to understand not just that cultural differences exist, but how it *feels* to experience the world differently, it may be easier to see how culture underlies all the other interesting things that make writers human—gender, status, experience, interest, will, resistance, character. It's tough and confusing to be a teacher these days, as the world grows closer.

Raj is sitting glumly in my office, staring at the fifth draft of a personal experience essay that he has titled "Problem Child." He hates this paper, he tells me. No matter what he does with it, it won't flow.

> *After living in the United States for a week, my sister-in-law admitted me in a nearby high school. My lack of knowledge and understanding of the English language caused me so much embarrassment and hardship in school that I wanted to go back to India. I had a hard time making friends here because of my language problems. At the end of my first year in school I had learned to speak fragmented English. I, however, was deficient in reading and comprehension. Music is a universal language.*

"I don't know how to connect this last sentence," he tells me. But this is the least of his problems. Raj is having a terrible, time understanding how to connect anything to a main point, to wind his thoughts around a central theme—"a point of tension," as his TA says in her notes on his paper. It's not a problem with logic. Within each section, each mini-story, the connections are there:

> *One day I was in a library and I came across a book called "Introduction to Psychology." I read the preface and understood very little, however I did comprehend the notion that psychology dealt with people and their behavior. After reading the preface I became very interested in psychology because I wanted to learn how to make new friends. I learned from the psychology book that in order to make new friends with other people I needed to have something in common with them.*

Raj and I have spent a lot of time talking about his life in order to find a central theme for this "self-analysis" paper. He seems to enjoy my questioning. "Did you always have trouble making friends, even in India?"

"Hm. Did I always have trouble making friends. I guess so, yes."

Raj is relaxed and smiling now, looking at me affectionately from behind his thick glasses. He may feel uncomfortable with his peers, but talking with family—brothers, cousins, nephews, aunts—is a passionately engaging activity in India, and his family is now far away.

"I never went out of the house much except for school," he continues. "My parents encouraged me, but I didn't really feel like it." He smiles, thinking back to his home village. "I did go out once, though, on a holiday when everyone flies kites. We had so much fun that day— the kite went up so high it completely disappeared. You know, it's *very* hard to bring down a kite when it's up that high," he tells me earnestly. There is such enjoyment in his face as he remembers those days that I am reluctant to stop him, even though I'm feeling a little impatient. I had been expecting this story to be an example of how he was a loner, even in India, but Raj has gotten diverted into the mechanics of kite flying, losing the thread, losing the point of what he was saying.

I continue my questioning, trying to refocus his attention so that we can work on that elusive central theme. I am hoping to find out just how he might have been different from other children in the neighborhood, and where those differences might have come from. "What did the other kids do after school?"

"Just hung around," he says.

"At tea stalls? Sweet shops?" I am thinking back, remembering my days in India. Raj gives a half nod after each of these possibilities, smiling in my direction. "But wait a minute," I remember, "that doesn't sound right." Kids like Raj wouldn't have been allowed to just hang around with street kids at tea stalls.

"At other kids' houses?" I ask. "Yes," he agrees. His voice is assertive, positive now. My mind flashes back to my Peace Corps service in India, to my exasperation with friends who were reluctant to give me a "no" for an answer when they thought I really wanted to hear a "yes," regardless of my need for information. "Will the bus leave soon?" "Yes, yes, right away." Hours later, the bus, which has had a flat tire that my companions knew about all along, finally pulls out of the terminal. It's amazing how much can flash back in the spaces within a conversation.

So, of course, middle-class boys spend time after school at the homes of their friends, not hanging around cheap tea stalls. I should have known this, since I have made much of the fact that I lived in

India, but Raj is too polite to emphasize my mistake by contradicting me. Instead, he has subtly, deftly, and completely unconsciously guided my understanding by his tone of voice and body language, even while giving me information that would mislead me if I hadn't learned, by experience fraught with bewilderment and frustration, how to interpret it.

Even though he has always felt uncomfortable around his peers, Raj is skilled at using subtle forms of communication in social situations. And it seems to me that the ability to use these nonverbal methods for giving information, internalized in childhood and perfected over eighteen years of intense social activity with extended family, is at least part of what is causing Raj so much trouble in his paper. Indeed, these politeness strategies are only the beginning of his repertoire of indirection; he also has a strong tendency to give the listener contextual information, stories that may seem unrelated to any main point, but which are intended to give the listener the *feel* of the situation, the context within which people act and by which their actions are understood. The kite incident, even though exemplifying the opposite of what I had been looking for, is part of the picture of his childhood, his life in his home town on the other side of the world. For people whose culture teaches that they can know something best when they immerse themselves in it, when they can feel—and thus experience— the complexities of all the relationships among people, things, and events, such contextual information is rich in possibilities for under-standing.[1]

But when Raj writes for the U.S. university, his audience finds such information beside the point, if not totally irrelevant. And his attempts to use these indirect communication strategies to fulfill his instructor's expectations that he build the story around a single point of tension create a sketchy series of unrelated incidents. His paper moves from his arrival in America to learning from a library book how to make new friends, to some background on the Top 40 (that they are songs played on the radio, that they are free for anyone to listen to, that most people listen to them "because most people aren't rich"), to some statistics on his home town in India, to the literacy and English skills of the farmers in the area, to Raj's own trouble making friends in his home town, to how he now tries to make friends through music.

When I look at the topics of these disconnected paragraphs, I realize that it might be possible to create a story line from them just as they are—a few transitional phrases, a few explicit statements of cause and effect, a little cut and paste—especially of "music is a universal language"—and all would be well. But what is both odd and telling is that Raj—hard as he tries—doesn't get it. I have suggested several ways of linking the parts directly, shown him how to make those smooth connections. But although Raj knows exactly where the links should be and can identify disjunctions easily without my help, he seems not to be able to keep the central theme in his mind long enough to weave his examples and facts and stories around it.

By now, Raj has no hope that he will ever really "learn to write," as he puts it. All he wants to do is get through the semester. It's gotten so that he is waiting outside my office when I come in the morning, hoping to catch me for a few minutes without an appointment. He is so agitated sometimes that I worry about him. I remember what a graduate student from Chile told me about how it feels to try to do something in writing that is contrary to what everything inside you is telling you to do. "When I tried to go straight to the point," she said, "I was putting things down that I didn't want to put. Every time I got the thoughts that were natural to me, I had to look for other ones. It felt as though I was being aggressive to myself. I was really mad sometimes, because I felt as if something was going against me."

The tendency to communicate through subtle implication, which is giving Raj such excruciating memories of his composition class, is shared by world majority students from cultures on every continent.[2] I learned of a particularly surprising similarity the summer I was training young Japanese stock-market analysts who had been sent to the U.S. by their employer to improve their English and gain some understanding of American culture. Part of our plan had been to introduce them to the idea of the U.S. as a multicultural society with various lifestyle choices, and so one weekend we packed them off to Provincetown on Cape Cod with a group of graduate students from Côte d'Ivoire. The West Africans and the Japanese took to each other readily, and by the end of the weekend they had discovered some interesting similarities in their cultures, including a sophisticated for-mality; a preference for subtle, indirect strategies in conversation; a deference to age, rank, and wisdom; and the use of roundabout strategies to show politeness.

"In my country, you don't say, 'Listen, I want to talk to you about this!'" said one of the Ivoirians, banging his fist on the table. "If you want to talk to me about something and you already said it, why should I listen any further? I'm going!" he said, getting up abruptly and walking to the door to emphasize his point. "You try to make a sort of suspense," he added, "and as we say: 'It brings appetite to the conversation,' you know? The person is thinking, 'What is he or she going to tell me?' And you really pull him to listen to you, you see?

And finally you say it. And by the time you say it, you are also at the end of what you are going to say."

A Japanese student told of how her respectful conversational style had caused her to be treated rudely by one of her undergraduate advisers at an exclusive U.S. college. "I still remember the day I walked into his office and started explaining about my papers, my ideas, what I would like to do, and he just cut me off. 'Stop beating around the bush! This is America! I have five minutes for you!' I was behaving out of my politeness, not to get into the issue right away, giving him the background first."

"Giving the background first" is, I would suggest, not only an oral strategy used in polite Japanese conversation between student and teacher, but a common way of communicating in both speech and writing in cultures around the world. Sarita, who gives stream-of-consciousness historical facts about her topic; Joseph, whose TA found the general remarks in his introduction "long-winded"; Raj, who gives the population figures for his natal village and details the different types of music on the Top 40; and the Kenyan doctoral student who thought to sketch the history and geography of his country before discussing curriculum revision, all are giving what they see as useful background for the reader to understand the topic properly. When I told Sarita that much of her introductory material would need to be cut, she nodded knowingly and said, "I guess here you assume that the reader has all the knowledge."

Sarita's assumption gives us an interesting insight into the difference between audience needs in a direct culture like our own and those in the cultures of the majority of the world that place more value on subtlety and context. In cultures that value directness, it is assumed that the reader needs to be shown exactly how any background information is tied to the ideas that the author wants to get across. Not only do we require transitional words and phrases and a careful, logical ordering of information, but we expect reminders of our previous points from one paragraph to the next, as well as careful emphasis on words that show precise and explicit relationships between ideas. Of course, even within the U.S. university there are styles of writing which are not as direct or explicit as what composition instructors expect in a basic academic argument. Writers of literary criticism, for example, can take more liberties than those in, say, political science or psychology. Journal articles in social anthropology or women's studies are generally more abstract and ornamental than the straightforward prose of biology or chemistry, which strives for correctness, simplicity, and dispassionate reporting of concrete detail even at the expense of reader interest.[3] But even in the writing of the more abstract disciplines at the U.S. university, there is an underlying *tendency* to directness, to precise relationships between verbs and their subjects, to clear and relatively obvious transitions, to announcements of intent and summary statements.

This tendency to explain everything, to make points and transitions and beginnings and endings obvious is not, then, a natural feature of "good writing." It *seems* natural because it is based on a straightforward style of oral communication used in many everyday interactions that is nonetheless relatively rare outside of western cultures. Though no style of communication is either completely explicit or completely implicit all of the time, in general it is fair to say that in western cultures, and especially in the U.S., children grow up with teachers, parents, and peers admonishing them to speak directly to the point and be relatively quick about it. "What are you driving at?" we ask when children digress. "Oh god, not another shaggy dog story!" "I don't get it." "Can you give me an example?" "So basically, what you're saying is. . . . " In "non western" cultures, however, children are taught from a very young age to present themselves and think about the world in quite different ways—myriad ways to be sure but, in general, ways that value subtlety.[4] Anthropologist Edward T. Hall (1976) draws a helpful distinction between high- and low-context cultural communication styles. In low-context cultures—mainly European, British, and U.S. mainstream—most of the information in the message must be made explicit, or, as I tell many world majority students, you need to talk to us the way you talk to a computer, leaving nothing to the imagination. In high-context cultures, on the other hand, much of the information in a message is not put into words at all, but is found, as Hall says, "either in the physical context or internalized in the person" (91). Like communication between twins who have grown up together, information transfer in high-context cultures relies on a good deal of a previous history of shared understanding and assumes that very little information is required, or even desired, for the audience to get the message.

Where these communication styles come from is a matter of conjecture: linguists point to the structure of various languages and their influence on thought and expression;[5] cross-cultural psychologists link genetic traits, the ecological environment, social structure, child-rearing practices, and dominant moral and religious thought to "character," which seems to include communication style;[6] classicists point out the differences between "oral" and "literate" societies and speculate about thought processes that may be developed through certain kinds of literacy and that lead, perhaps, to particular communication styles.[7] Scollon and Scollon, in their study of Athabaskan discourse strategies, point out that the western need for clarity, even transparency, in written communication dates back to the Protestant Reformation, when language came to be seen as "the clear reflection of the orderliness of the natural world"; any prose that was "unclear, contextual, symbolic or not strictly grammatical was judged as . . . an offense to God's natural law" (1981, 44). But while this was going on in Europe, cultures unaffected by the Protestant reform movement continued to place an emphasis on social and rhetorical conditions, on the beauty and sophistication of suggestion, on multiple interpretations.

These worldwide strategies of indirection—linguistic, rhetorical, poetic, psychological—create a richness that to world majority students makes the spare, relentless logic of the western tradition seem meager in comparison. "When I read something written by an American it sounds so childish," confessed a graduate student from Chile. "It's because we don't see with these connections. It's just like: 'This is a watch, the watch is brown, da-da, da-da.' For us, that's funny. I think that for Americans, it must be funny, the way I describe things."

A Brazilian student writes about the three visits she made to the U.S. before she enrolled in a master's program:

> There is something difficult about being in a different culture, or just speaking a foreign language, that is "appropriateness." In my opinion that is one of the hardest issues in coping with differences. When is the right time to say "hello," or "hi," or start a conversation? When to ask personal questions or just be indifferent? When and under what circumstances is it appropriate to do such and such? Basically, human beings are the same, and have more or less the same potential attitudes, knowledge and skills. So why are they so diverse? I think that what changes is the composition of the different elements or the way they are structured based on facts and circumstances. For instance, Americans say "Time is money," and money in a capitalist system is something to be saved or invested in productivity. It sounds crazy, but I think this idea can change the whole concept of time and the way it is spent in a society. Time and space are two abstract concepts that are lived by the way they are defined. I do not know what comes first, the system, the cultural values, or the people, but whatever order they have, they seem to be inter-related somehow. So if I have to make a stereotype of how American culture appears to me, I would say it is rational, dry, left-brain oriented, individualistic, values individual initiative and individual freedom, self-centered and proud of itself.
> The third time I came to the U.S . . .

In this characteristically digressive style of expression, the writer does not necessarily feel the weight of responsibility to "make sense";

in fact, this student and others told me that it is more the responsibility of the *audience* to do the analysis, to get the gist, to draw meaning from the context. But it is important to realize, students say, that the audience is not expected to have complete freedom of interpretation; instead, the speaker or writer is supposed to give so much context, to say the same thing in so many different ways, that the audience finally gets the message that the speaker is trying to convey. This is done out of respect for the reader or listener: "You don't want to depress your audience by giving everything away immediately," they say, "leaving nothing for them to do. And you don't want to bore them, either, so you do what is considered interesting, which is to give plenty of details and a conversational tone to your written text."[8]

But the word "conversational" needs to be taken in context, for conversation in one language and culture may be very different from what it is in another. In Spanish or Portuguese, for example, speakers and writers may be verbose, rambling, digressive, holistic, full of factual details, full of feeling, sometimes repetitious, sometimes contradictory, without much concern for literal meanings. In many Asian and African languages and cultures, metaphor, euphemism, innuendo, hints, insinuation, and all sorts of subtle nonverbal strategies—even silence—are used both to spare the listeners possible embarrassment or rejection and to convey meanings that they are expected to grasp.[9] In Japanese, for example, there are sixteen ways to avoid saying "no";[10] in Arabic, a host of euphemisms designate the touchy subjects that no one wants to speak of directly; in Sinhalese, indirection takes the form of metaphors or universal symbols to which can be added prefixes or suffixes to create a poetic mood or feeling. In Korean, verbs may be passive where we might expect them to be active. *"One of my most interesting experiences was working in the cardiology department where I received direct patient interaction,"* writes a medical school applicant who came to the U.S. when she was two. "People don't understand how Korean we are at home," she tells me in perfect English. "I've always had trouble with writing." *"There is no way I can apologize for my poor academic performance in my first year,"* she continues in the "personal statement" that she has brought for my corrections. "What I mean," she says, "is that the transition from a small girl's school to the University of Michigan was a disaster."

I raise an eyebrow. "Why don't you say so?"

"I am crossed between two cultures," she says ruefully.

Edgardo, a first-year student from Puerto Rico, brings me a paper which, while not as disjointed as Raj's "Problem Child," still has a definite need for transitions. He listens to my explanation of the needs of the U.S. university audience, but when he brings his paper back for me to look at his corrections, some of the transitions look as if they have been lifted from a list without much attention to their meanings. He uses "furthermore" when he needs something like "however" or "although," and strings various thoughts together without attention to parallelism, without sorting them out into the neat categories I am expecting. He laughs at himself a little when I tell him this, for he knows that it's not that he hasn't thought about his argument or that he has difficulty thinking logically; rather, the idea of having to find the exact words to express the precise, almost mathematical relationships between ideas is not nearly as important to him as it is to me. As we look at each of his transitions, trying to determine the meaning he wants to convey, I tell him, as I have told students from so many different cultures: "You have to be *extremely* literal in this context." When I say this, Edgardo's usually patient face betrays a glimmer of exasperation. "You can't give the reader credit for *anything* here," he says.

The status that students hold in their home countries can add another twist to students' writing strategies. An older Nepali graduate student, for example, told me that although he is a published writer and holds a respectable government position, he is still the youngest male in his family and is "junior to everybody." As a consequence, he says, "I have to obey everybody, so I don't have that loud voice, I don't have that strong vocabulary in my writing. I always try to be very polite, humble, keep very low. But here at the U.S. university, you have to find words that will voice your opinion very strongly. You have to find words that will give a lot of contrast. You have to find words that will show that you are very aggressive. So I had to learn this vocabulary, and you can imagine how frustrated I was with that." But higher status does not necessarily mean a greater tendency to be direct. For well-placed officials (who may come to the U.S. as graduate students or visiting scholars), or for members of elite families, or for older, more dominant siblings, getting down to business quickly or giving one's own opinion forcefully or immediately in a discussion may be considered unsophisticated. In many cultures, the most dominant members of a group sit back and listen to the others debate and discuss, perhaps adding a few well-chosen comments at the end, rather than entering the discussion early on and making their views clearly known, as is more common in U.S. culture. When such students are then required to adopt the opposite strategies in writing, especially writing in which their own views or their own interpretation of their research is supposed to be presented, they may feel understandably strange about making themselves look foolish.

For some students, these cultural tendencies toward indirectness can be even more accentuated by political necessity.[11] Kamala, my friend from Sri Lanka, showed me a paper based on lengthy interviews she had done of government officials while working in southern Africa which had been reviewed unfavorably by her graduate adviser. As I read it, I could see why, for she had left out whole sections of the interviews that contained her most revealing data, though her conclusions hinted at this material and suggested that what she had left out was clear proof of her claim—although the claim itself was also unclear. Talking about this paper with Kamala was a lengthy process, both because of her subtle, refined conversational style and because she was reluctant to talk about the politically sensitive material at all, even in a context that seemed far removed from any possible repercussions. When she assured me that all these data were there in her interview notes—very important data—I told her that she needed to at least mention it; perhaps she could talk about why she had chosen to leave out direct quotations. But Kamala found even this an unnaturally direct way of dealing with the problem, and her final draft contained little more than what she had originally included, confirming her professor's unfortunate impression that she was an underprepared student whose inability to "learn to write" would seriously compromise her graduate studies.

In another case of cultural confusion, Ting Han, a first-year student from Singapore, was extremely upset about the way we had judged his performance on the entrance assessment, which asked him to establish and support a position on how educational priorities should be set in difficult economic times. Ting had learned to write under the British system of competitive examinations, he told me, and had done quite well there. He had been taught to explore different sides of an issue, just as he had done in his essay.

"But Ting, you needed to take a position," I told him. "It's not enough to just give some pros and cons."

"But that was intentional. I don't want to take a position!" In Singapore, he explained, you would never state your opinion directly on such a topic; you might be arrested. Because of the great variety of people, cultures, religions that coexist on the small island, he told me, the government must be strict, and everyone understands that it is better to be diplomatic. Then, too, Singapore has powerful neighbors to think about. It can't go on giving its opinion directly, as neighboring countries are quick to take offense. One has to be careful.

Even more interesting to me was Ting's interpretation of how students would respond to any mention of educational priorities by the authorities:

> *Critics will argue against setting educational priorities because they restrict a person's options in choosing his interested field of study. Hence, it is a violation against a person's freedom. The educational system, by setting priorities, will enforce the people to take up courses that are of no interest to them. Consequently, the people may lose interest and give up on their studies. Instead of improving the country's prosperity, it will cause a social problem for the country.*

Ting and I talked about this passage for some time before I realized what he wasn't telling me directly: that if a country like Singapore were to set educational priorities at all, it would be sending a subtle message to students that it wanted them to go heavily into certain fields of study. Thus it would be laying an uncomfortable burden of obligation on students who were interested in other areas, but who would nevertheless feel compelled to study the subjects the government seemed to recommend. In a high-context culture that is influenced by Confucianism, which emphasizes mutual obligations and a strong sense of duty to parents, teachers, and the state, the authorities need only to hint for students to understand what they are obligated to do. Even though Ting knew he was writing for a different audience, and even mentioned in his paper some possible differences in educational priorities that might be set for the U.S. as opposed to Singapore, he had no idea that U.S. students might not react to subtle pressure from authorities in the same way as students from Confucian cultures. He was very interested when I told him this, and we talked a little about child-rearing differences and the cultural necessity of directness in this context. After we had talked for a while, I suggested that what he might have done in his essay was to tell us that students in Singapore would interpret the setting of priorities as a strong message from the government and that they would then feel obligated to do what they were told. At this suggestion, Ting laughed, incredulous at the degree of explicitness required. Even though he now understood something more about the needs of his new audience, such a strategy seemed unnecessarily—even stupidly—elaborate to him.

Ting from a Chinese culture, Edgardo from a Latin one, and Raj from India, all are struggling with the same problem: understanding— even *believing*—the necessity for "transparent" communication in their new cultural context. For whatever reason, perhaps maturity, perhaps political naïveté, it is Edgardo who is responding the most rapidly to my suggestions for change. Now that he feels my respect for his background, now that he understands that I see his vagueness as a perfectly reasonable way of communicating, he is listening hard to my insistence on literal meanings in this new context, my exaggeration of the boxlike format I want him to use to organize his ideas. In the space of three weeks, his papers are showing a marked change. My only fear now is that he will escape from my class and our one-on-one conversations about writing too soon—that he will go out into the world with a caricature of the five-paragraph essay tucked so firmly under his belt that his future instructors will throw up their hands and tell him he is writing like a high school student. I need a little more time to help him learn how to fill in the boxes with the complex ideas he has always had in his head, to convince him that I am not trying to reduce his writing to a simplistic statement of either A or B, but that within the framework that makes sense to his new audience there is room, even invitation, to explore.

Edgardo will learn quickly. But he may be an exception. More often, students seem to take much longer to catch on—if they do catch on at all. I had recommended that Ting be placed into a regular composition section after a semester of introductory work on academic argument despite his continuing difficulties, for his pride seemed hurt by his placement. But soon he was doing poorly again and was back in Writing Workshop, angry, scared, and still not convinced that he needed to think about his audience in a radically different way. Raj, meanwhile, has turned in his self-analysis essay, having smoothed the transitions somewhat, but still, after three times the effort of most students, never having figured out how to relate the title "Problem Child" to anything specific in the paper. Raj's difficulties are particularly acute because he is so new to this culture—he came only five years ago without a word of English—and because of his traditional up-bringing in a small village, unusual for a student who after only a few years of U.S. high school has been accepted at an elite U.S. university. And we must add to that his difficulty in making friends, which has kept him isolated from American culture and, as a consequence, fairly oblivious to the needs of a western audience. ("*I like to be alone because I want to have a peaceful mind,*" he writes on one of his drafts. "*I am also satisfied with myself alone.*")

To add to the already complex picture, Raj is an engineering major and, like other "gearheads," is much more at home doing math problems or reviewing his chemistry notes than he is writing a self-analysis. Some of my U.S. students who are mathematically oriented also have difficulty with four-page essays, which in their case has nothing to do with a cultural tendency to indirection. I ask Kevin, who is working on a paper called "Jackson Pollack—Are His Paintings Really Art?" to give me his opinion on which is more intellectually demanding, his preintroductory composition course or calculus, which he is taking simultaneously. "Oh, composition, for sure," he says. "In math, you just have to concentrate on one thing after another. That comes naturally to me. When you write a paper, you have to view the whole thing at once. That's tough."

At first this may seem contradictory. As we have seen, most "non western" societies are holistic; they emphasize and value how things are interconnected, the roles that people play, the relationships they have to each other and to the natural world. In such a system, you can't understand something very well in isolation, in the abstract; thus the tendency is for speakers or writers to give contextual and emotional information, to fill the audience in on the big picture, to help them feel the way the author felt in such a situation. In other words, they "view the whole thing at once," which, according to Kevin, is especially hard for someone who tends to see the trees instead of the forest.

But I think the "whole thing" that Kevin is talking about is different from the contextual whole that Raj sees and wants to help his audience experience through indirect, information-rich strategies. What Kevin finds hard is exactly what is bothering Raj—keeping a central theme, a point of tension in mind at the same time he is trying to think of a line of reasoning that weaves in and out of it. But give Kevin the strategies and he sees what he needs to do. "I like your idea of putting my thesis statement on the wall over my computer," Kevin tells me. "That way I don't get lost in my argument." It seems to work for him; just a few meetings, a few suggestions, and he is on his way. Putting together a written argument is still hard for him, but at least he knows what the task is, and the task makes sense to him. Regardless of his predilection for small mathematical details, he has been surrounded by direct, relatively sparse messages all his life, from TV commercials to sit-com scripts to dinner-table admonitions to "get to the point" of the stories he tells. It may be tough for him to keep all the strings together while weaving them into a pattern, but his culture tells him that a pattern needs to be there, and it gives him the guidelines within which he must contain his thinking if the pattern is to "make sense."[12]

But Raj comes from a context where tightly woven connections between ideas and support, center and periphery, background and thesis are not what is important. What's important is seeing, feeling, and being situated in the web of relationships that surround and permeate the subject, and finding pleasure in the process. "When I came to the U.S.," says Raj in his final draft, "I was astounded by American culture." No wonder.

3 "In Solidarity": The Voice of the Collectivity

I agree, and I believe most people do, that one should marry whom he or she loves. Yet, if the couple were from different races, many would disagree with me. For instance, Malcolm X, in his autobiography, refers to the relationship between mixed couples as being entirely sexual, lacking in love and with complete disrespect between partners. This is the idea most Americans have regarding interracial marriage. However, that idea is refuted by several couples who were invited by Newsweek magazine to comment on Spike Lee's <u>Jungle Fever</u> and the issues it raises. These couples allude to their marriage as lovely and truthful, with the same common problems that other marriages have.

Tony is sitting in my office, on the side of the desk that I leave deep in shadows. He seems comfortable there; while I read the beginning of his paper aloud, he glances around at the collection on my walls— two photographs, taken from different angles, of a statue of a crowd in Montreal, a long piece of indigo batik, hand-dyed by a friend in Togo, a map of the Americas printed upside down.

"This is the idea most Americans have regarding interracial marriage," I read again, slowly. "Why do you say that?" Tony is from Angola and has been in the States for only a few months. He is smiling slightly, as he always does, his eyes gentle and expectant. I lean back in my chair and wait a long time for his response.

"I inferred this because I saw the movie *Jungle Fever,*" Tony says finally. His voice is soft, almost inaudible, but there is no hesitancy there. He is sure, quite sure, that his idea about Americans is correct.

"Mm." I think about this for a minute, this discrepancy between "most Americans" and the views of a few people interviewed about a depressing, controversial film. Tony lets me think. He sits quietly, watching my face. I screw up my eyes and shake my head a little, trying to understand it. "How can you generalize from the movie?" I ask. Tony is silent. "You need to provide some support for your view. Maybe you're right, maybe most Americans really do think this way. But you need to be explicit about why you think this is true."

In conference the following week, Tony shows me his second draft:

For instance, Malcolm X, in his autobiography, refers to the relationship between mixed couples as being entirely sexual, lacking in love and

> *with complete disrespect between partners. This is the idea most*
> *Americans have regarding interracial marriage. Great evidence of this*
> *is the film, Jungle Fever, where Spike Lee seems to be speaking through*
> *the eyes of a common black man, and presents the same idea as*
> *Malcolm X did almost 30 years ago.*

"Now here," I point to his paper, "here you say 'through the eyes
of a common black man.' That's a bit of a contradiction for me." I
look at Tony; he is watching me carefully. "Because up here, you make
a statement about what "most people" believe, and down here, where
you give your evidence, you talk about the common black man." "Oh,"
says Tony, nodding. Tony has been sent to the U.S. by his country's
national oil company to study computer science. He is a bit older than
my other first-year students; he has already done several years of
college in Angola.

"If you are going to talk about 'most Americans,' that would
include . . . " I glance sideways at Tony, "black women . . . ?" Tony
raises his eyebrows in pleased surprise. "White women? White men?"
"Yes, I see." Tony is nodding more firmly now.

Now that he seems to understand my point about overgeneralizing,
I start to work out a way to explain to him the difficulties of using
the views of first Malcolm X, and then Spike Lee and Malcolm X, as
evidence of what most people think, but something stops me. Tony's
apparent confusion about "most people" and "the common black
man" seems like a simple error in logic, but this computer science
major, who finds his calculus class "easy," did not catch it. Is there
something I am not understanding?

Before this occurred to me, I thought fleetingly that Tony, being a
newcomer, was simply making a judgment about how Americans must
think on the basis of his first impressions. This, of course, is a common
mistake of sojourners in a new society. When I made my first trip to
Africa, as a trainer of Peace Corps volunteers, I made such mistakes
daily, despite nearly twenty years of living in other people's cultures,
despite my distrust of surface impressions. But there had been something in Tony's eyes, something in his initial, quiet certainty about
what most Americans think . . .

I look at the page again. "Great evidence of this is the film *Jungle
Fever.*" Why does he emphasize that—great evidence? Then suddenly,
I realize my mistake. Of course. I was seeing this paper through the
eyes of my own society. "Tony, I think this is a really interesting
cultural difference. Tell me if you think my idea is correct."

Tony sits up a bit straighter, there in the shadows, listening carefully.
"It seems to me that in your society, when a famous person speaks,

that person speaks for everyone, in a way. When a filmmaker makes a movie, or when someone speaks at a public assembly, they are saying what the whole society believes." Tony nods, but his eyes retreat a little. He is familiar with the colonialist argument that his people are childishly inclined to agree with whatever their leaders tell them. I feel his resistance; I recognize it from conversations with many friends and research informants from developing countries. But I push on, anyway.

"And because yours is a collectivist culture, public figures really can speak for everyone, in solidarity, is that right?" At that word— "solidarity"—Tony's eyes brighten. He is nodding, interested that I know this, a little relieved. "Of course I'm well aware that people in a collectivity still have their own opinions," I say, smiling, making a show of my own naïveté in stating the obvious. Tony starts to laugh quietly, nodding in delight.

"But here, the society is more individualistic," I continue. Tony's expression immediately turns serious and attentive. He has heard this before about Americans, of course, but now he is just becoming aware of its implications. "And so," I continue, "when Spike Lee says something in a film, people will say that he just speaks for Spike Lee. Now since he is controversial, and artistic, and therefore probably has something insightful to say about human behavior, he undoubtedly does speak for more people than just himself. But most of us would not assume that he speaks for everyone." "Oh," says Tony. This is not just an "oh" of acceptance any more. It's an "oh" of something a little closer to understanding, even though this idea of individualism is confusing for him.

"So if I understand this right, " I tell him, "when you said the film was evidence that all Americans thought this way about intermarriage, you were assuming that the ideas about evidence we have here are the same as those in your country." Tony is nodding, looking at me quizzically. "If they were, then Spike Lee's message really would be appropriate evidence for this paper, wouldn't it? And 'the common black man' would also include the rest of us?"

This twist is a little too much for either of us to grasp, for we both have been thinking about the paper in terms of our own views of reality, and now, for a moment, we are trying to look at the thing through both cultural lenses simultaneously. From an individualist viewpoint, "what most people believe" would have to be documented with polls and percentages or many more citations of text and film in order to be certain that "most people" really hold a particular opinion. From a collectivist standpoint, however, what is important is the appearance of unity, not the obvious logical inconsistency that may lie behind it. I am reminded of a picture in a book for international development workers in which the government census taker in a collectivist culture is asking a group of local people, "How many of you are there?" The villagers are lined up, linked arm in arm: the old man, the child, the man with the hoe, the adolescent, the woman with baby in arms. "We are one," they answer.[1]

To understand the idea of collectivism a little more clearly, let's shift for a moment to a totally different culture, one that is not even "non western," but, because it is an ancient culture in America, has many of the characteristics of the cultures of the world majority. Rural Québec in the 1970s and 1980s, when I lived and raised my children there, was in some ways still as closely woven as it had been in the seventeenth century, when French Jesuit priests, alarmed by the effects of the Reformation in Europe, embarked to the New World, where they could preach their version of the gospel to the fur traders and farmers who came to settle in the fertile plains of the St. Lawrence Valley. The settlers were soon joined by "Les Filles du Roi" or "the King's Daughters," eight hundred destitute young women from Parisian orphanages who were rounded up by a magnanimous Louis XIV and sent to New France to marry and bear children.

Throughout the next two centuries, the emphasis on farming, piety, and reproduction remained; the small farms produced food in abundance, and every farm family was attended to by a village priest whose combination of paternalistic vigilance, powerful authority, and genuine concern for the maintenance of tradition ensured that each family did its duty: seventeen, twenty-two, even thirty live births per household were not unheard of even in the 1950s. Education was limited, especially for boys, who were needed for the heaviest farm labor, and advancement of a bright young man into any profession other than the traditional "four notables"—clergy, notary, doctor, or small merchant—was almost impossible in a society dominated by both the English, who had barred the door to any more lucrative or intellectual occupations for the French majority, and by the tiny political, cultural, and religious French elite, who feared any disturbance of the social order. The resulting combination of low literacy rates and general conservatism among a preoccupied and somewhat cowed population helped maintain the close-knit collectivism of a society so isolated from its English Canadian and U.S. neighbors by its language, culture, and long history of oppression.[2]

Even after Québec's "Quiet Revolution" of the 1960s, with its sweeping educational reforms, its drastic drop in birth rate (at 1.3

children per family, now one of the lowest in the world), and its sudden and massive rejection of the excesses of the clergy, much of the collectivist tradition remains. The countryside is still a network of families with similar last names; the Bourbonnais and the Farands and the Leroux can all trace their ancestral roots down winding roads to their neighbors' farms. The postmistress will tell you that her son-in-law's mother was born in the little house beside the railroad tracks and that her grandchildren live across the road in the house with the swimming pool. Her husband's cousin (whom she'd rather not discuss because she's not speaking to her at the moment) lives in the mobile home parked on the parcel of land she got from her elderly father, who, with only a fifth-grade education, has been the town's mayor for years. She'll tell you that the little man riding the child-sized bicycle is the town dwarf—don't mind his rude comments, he shouts them at everybody. He's been sleeping in the post office ever since he ran away from the old people's home, but nobody's offended, even when he gets dressed in front of the window. He ran away to the church once and demanded that they take him in, but when the sisters tried to give him a bath, he ran away again.

Children in rural Québec still grow up surrounded by adoring aunts and uncles, skipping to Grandma's house for lunch on school days, riding tractors into the fields with their fathers when they are small and taking over the controls themselves by the time they're ten, hunting wild garlic in the woods in the spring and cross-country skiing out their kitchen doors in the winter. They have little time for friends on weekends and holidays, for such days are reserved for entertaining relatives on a grand scale. The grandparents, the cousins, the brothers-and sisters-in-law, the aunts and uncles (some of them still only babies), all gather at one house or another to renew the bonds of family—the backbone of community. Everyone comes ready to have a good time, ready to mute the tensions and hurt feelings that inevitably spring up between family members, ready to slip into a comfortable, joking mood and enjoy the simple pleasures of gossip, and good food, and the same old card games, for group attachment and communication are far more important here than personal pride, or politics, or principle. Every weekend, every holiday, this collectivist society talks and laughs together, cementing the ties between generations. They listen to the music of Elvis and the new American rock stars, and sometimes they turn off the stereo and get out the fiddle or the harmonica and spoons and then everyone—teenagers, grandparents, five-year-olds—sings the old folk songs late into the night.

School, too, is a friendly place, now that the reforms of the 1960s have torn away the brittle crust of oppression, the everyday indignities practiced by petty administrators on teachers, and teachers, in their turn, on children. Out from underneath this thin, repressive hierarchy, an egalitarian spirit has emerged, a family spirit still sharp in living memory from the days when huge families lived packed together through the long bitter winters, sharing the labor, amusing each other, finding ways to get along.

Nowadays one still finds an extraordinary group spirit, a kind of cheering for everybody, that is foreign to individualistic Americans. The day of the Christmas concert, for example, my neighbor's ten-year-old appeared at school wearing a skirt and an old undershirt. Her parents had left home early to visit her brother in the hospital, and their daughter had grabbed the first articles of clothing at hand so as not to miss the school bus. As she filed to the front of the auditorium with the rest of her class, flashing me a smile of recognition as she passed, it was clear that she was not in the least embarrassed by her faux pas, and, even more startling, there was not so much as a snicker from the entire elementary school audience, many of whom were dressed in the latest teen fashions.

At the same concert, a dancer waited on stage while her record was put on three times in the wrong place, but she was no more concerned about this than if she had been practicing in her own living room. A boy in a white suit did a pretty fair imitation of Elvis, and although he was cheered wildly by a contingent of fifth-grade girls, there was no great difference between the response he was given and the applause for the second grader who struggled through a recorder solo of "Clair de lune."

If you should happen to visit Québec on a Friday night and stop in at a small town shopping mall, you would see the usual crowds of blue-jeaned youth standing around in little groups, deep in conversation about the usual teenage concerns. But in contrast to the scene in similar shopping malls in the U.S., there is remarkably little separation between the generations. A young couple with a baby walks by a group of teenagers and they all turn to look at the baby and smile, and take its hand and include it in their group for a moment. An old man shuffles by, and the adolescents recognize him as someone's grand-uncle and find a way to laugh with him—not merely out of respect for their elders, but because he is family.

Go up to a counter at a village store and you will hear customers joking with the cashier, the meat man, the bag boy, joking about anything, always the same banal subject matter, the same phrases, jokes everyone has heard many times before, and at the punch line, the speaker will inevitably turn toward you as if to a co-conspirator, and laugh, meeting your eyes for a moment—this small gesture so unexpected, so friendly, so conducive to solidarity.

But at the same time that children are raised to include everyone and to value everyone's efforts equally, they are also inured to a certain acceptance of sameness that seems odd to Americans used to a faster pace, a greater variety of choices. At Halloween, I learned, you give out only certain items: miniature candy bars, home-grown apples (though the kids never eat them), little bags of chips, small change, peanuts in the shell. Nobody has ever heard of popcorn balls; you don't waste your time baking cupcakes or spend your money on bubble gum or licorice ropes or any of the other goodies that in U.S. towns make a kid's Halloween bag a treasure trove for months to come.

Once I made orange-frosted cookies, but nobody knew what to do with them. The kids were absolutely stumped. They didn't want to put them into their bags, for of course they would get crushed and smear frosting all over everything. So why not eat them right away? A little quick energy for the long tramp to the next farmhouse? The smaller kids giggled and bit right in, but the older children found the novelty disturbing. Only after much hesitation did they consent to my startling suggestion, and even then, they ate slowly, without enthusiasm. The next year I went back to miniature candy bars and throw-away apples, and everyone breathed freely again.

It isn't that the rural society lacks imagination; in fact, it can be enormously creative. The most fantastic creatures would appear at my kitchen door on Halloween night: a boy with a third leg, a half-man-half-woman, a little old fiddler you would have sworn was at least fifty, two tiny fat gnomes, an overgrown baby. But when the imagination occupies a fitting and proper place in the scheme of things, minds that can create strikingly original costumes without the help of store-bought patterns also balk at the strangeness of biting into an orange-frosted cookie on Halloween when Cookies Aren't Done.

In such a society, where the group is close-knit and no one's contribution is derided or envied; where everyone does the same things and shares the same aspirations (rural teenage girls, with remarkable regularity, say they want to be hairdressers, while the boys want to be auto mechanics); where everyone expects to live just down the road from their parents all their lives and entire extended families will rent a hall and gather on New Year's, hundreds of them; where grandmothers still hold the role of oral historians, remembering the names of everyone to invite, remembering the marriages, the deaths, the new arrivals; in such a society there develops a sense of common knowledge, common ideas and opinions that do not have to be explicitly stated to be understood.

Imagine, now, variations on this society around the world. From a Japanese corporate board room to a teacher's lounge in Côte d'Ivoire to a gathering of women washing clothes in a river in rural Ecuador to the corporate culture of IBM subsidiaries in Guatemala or Pakistan or Taiwan or Thailand,[3] what is important is harmony, consensus, and the *appearance*, at least, of unity. Although the history, the languages, the details of the traditions are all quite different, the feeling and expectation of connectedness are the same. In contrast to our emphasis on individual effort and personal success, where children learn to think of themselves as "I" instead of "we," where shades of individual opinion are carefully studied and singled out for praise or criticism, collectivist societies teach that in group harmony lie security, contact, comfort, and identity.

Collectivists, looking at individualist societies, often find them cold and selfish. This is one of the first bitter comments made by many world majority students soon after they arrive in the U.S. People move so fast, dwell so fleetingly on conversation and relationships that personal ties seem to mean nothing here. Like Alexis de Tocqueville, who came as a young man in the 1830s to study American democracy, many students coming to the U.S. from collectivist cultures are both admiring and condemnatory of the individualism that democracy fosters and would agree that such a society not only "make[s] every man forget his ancestors, but it hides his descendants and separates his contemporaries from him; it throws him back forever upon himself alone and threatens in the end to confine him entirely within the solitude of his own heart" (de Tocqueville 1990, 99).

Imagine, then, what it must be like to come from a collectivist society to a U.S. university where your ideas about togetherness are turned on their heads. Imagine your instructor, like Joseph's, telling you in a voice clearly marked by irritation that the way you are envisioning harmony is wrong, wrong, wrong.

> Joseph—I tried telling you this before, and I can't stress it enough: you just *can't pull phrases and expressions* from a writer's text and use them without *quoting* them! This is true not just for whole sentences but for phrases like "inexplicable continuity" or even particular word choices, like "chaotic" or "regularity," which represent an author's choice among the various ways he or she might have expressed something. To use an author's words in

this way, without quoting them, is simply against the rules, like serving over the table in ping pong, only worse. Lots of people even think it's unethical, a sort of intellectual theft. Whether or not you think of it that way, you need to know that you just can't do this in academic writing, and can get in a lot of trouble if you do. Understand?

But Joseph does not understand. In a world where your thoughts, feelings, and experiences are inextricably connected to those of others, why would it be so important to sort out whose idea is whose? When the words of others may be so similar to your own sometimes that they might be said to *be* your own, then isn't it a little exaggerated to say that using somebody's particular word choice constitutes "theft"?

It's not that Joseph doesn't understand the rules of correct documentation, or that he doesn't grasp the *concept* of rules as his instructor, in her frustration, implies, or that he hasn't heard that appropriating the ideas of others could get him into trouble. He has heard all this many times before about writing in the U.S. academic context, and he has probably nodded and said that he understood. But he is not convinced. Everything in his life has always been connected in subtle and diverse ways with everything and everyone else, and now it must somehow become separate, in ways that he may not even approve of. And what is even harder to accept is that the shift he is being asked to make is put to him in terms of rules about good writing, rules that he must adopt if he wants to appear smart and well prepared. Joseph balks at this, and rightly so, because this issue is not about intelligence, not about correctness. It has to do with something deeper and more fundamental, something to do with values and how one conceives of oneself as a human being. Of course, the experience of individualism is not totally foreign to collectivist ways of thinking, for feeling part of a harmonious group and feeling like a separate individual are both worldwide human experiences; it is the *emphasis* that is different, and that emphasis, that difference in perception of what is most valued, results in an entirely different look and feel to the world, creating a gulf between the two kinds of societies that is at the same time extremely difficult to perceive and perilous to cross.[4]

It is this cultural emphasis on collectivism, I would suggest, that so deeply affects Joseph's writing and thinking about writing, just as it affects Tony's ideas about evidence. In this paper of Joseph's and in his conversations with his instructor, this effect of culture manifests itself as a formidable resistance to correct documentation, but in other papers, his collectivist values and communication style affect his writing and thinking in quite different ways. In a personal piece, for example,

Joseph introduces his subject with elaborate strategies that sound like the lengthy oral introductions so necessary in his own West African society: the long, drawn-out commonplaces; the inquiries after the family; the warm, lingering handshakes—all the warmer as friends grow closer; the sympathetic tone the voice takes on, almost musical, like a reed instrument, harmonizing, empathizing. In this way, speakers draw each other into the dialogue, creating each time anew the feeling of community; only after this effect is achieved can true communication begin.

Here is Joseph's one-page introduction to a three-page paper he calls "The Displacement of My Ping-Pong Bat and Myself," an introduction that his U.S. instructor found "long-winded," something to be cut, drastically, so that the point may become apparent sooner, but which to Joseph is a necessary part of setting the mood for a sympathetic reading and a heart-to-heart understanding:

The Displacement of My Ping-Pong Bat and Myself

Honor, fame, respect, recognition and love: these are scarce commodities which most humans long for but which accompany only a few distinguished and talented members of any society. Powerful politicians, music superstars, college and professional athletes, academic legends, military warriors and beauty queens all move around with the above commodities. Even when we do not fall into the above categories, we still could enjoy a significant amount of all of these things in our families and little neighborhoods where everybody knows our names.

The subject of this paper is displacement as it relates to my ping pong bat and myself. There are only a few people on earth who have not suffered from it in their lives. It comes in different ways and could be very frustrating and disheartening when not properly handled. Take for instance an only child who has the attention of his or her family. Guess what? Suddenly a new baby comes along, diverting the family's attention to the new member. Most people I know have almost gone insane dealing with this displacement.

What about beauty queens who lost their crowns because some better looking woman came on the scene? I have seen some of them decline terribly as they resort to a solitary kind of life. The same thing applies to boxers who, while resisting another kind of displacement, become insane due to deadly and devastating blows to the head sustained during resistance.

The point I am trying to make here is that if you have not suffered from displacement, you will someday, and when it does come to you, I want you to remember my paper and not forget the old adage which says "no condition is permanent."

In the light of the above, I am going to commence writing this essay presuming that we all have at least once in our lives felt recognized, respected and loved. I will also, at this juncture, presume

*that you will be able to understand after reading my essay, why my
ping pong bat and myself feel displaced.*
*In Nigeria where I come from, the game of table tennis is a very
popular sport . . .*

Finally, Joseph has established the mood to his satisfaction, and now
begins the essay proper with a story about his own experience as a
nationally renowned ping-pong player coming to the U.S., where his
fame is unrecognized.

In collectivist cultures, unifying rhetoric is put to many different
uses; it can put the audience in a mood of harmony, as Joseph's
introduction illustrates, or it can be used to coax the audience into
going along with a particular position or to chide dissenters back into
the fold.[5] This valuing of social solidarity sometimes shows up in
student writing in the form of rhetorical questions and a tendency to
gloss over specifics that might raise questions or doubts. For example,
Milton, a sophomore from Hong Kong, has written a paper that argues
in favor of repatriating the Vietnamese boat people from the refugee
camps in his country.

*Thousands of boats with tens of thousands of refugees departed from
Vietnam and started their voyage to the capitalist cities in the South
China Sea. As a result, Hong Kong became a major asylum in east
Asia. From then onwards, Hong Kong had to accommodate Vietnamese
at an average of fifty thousand people every year. That is almost one
percent of the entire population of Hong Kong! There is no doubt that
Hong Kong needed to be human and accommodate these Vietnamese.
However, one percent of the population is unfair, isn't it? Doesn't it
exceed the limits of humanitarianism? As Hong Kong is already one
of the ten densest cities in the world, I could become a super millionaire
if I found a good site for an extra one percent of the population. Let
alone an open site for five hundred weekend campers.*

Milton's sense of humor goes a long way with me; his voice is so
lively, his prose so direct and clear—far superior, in that respect, to
many of my U.S. mainstream students—that I hesitate to insist that
he completely rethink his style. However, for an individualist audience—at least an individualist *academic* audience—he really does need
to assume an entirely different purpose for his writing. Instead of
trying to create consensus through a good-natured appeal to reasonableness ("c'mon guys, give us a break, we're doing the best we can"),
he would have to change tactics entirely and try to convince his
audience by presenting a careful examination of the evidence that
readers could weigh for themselves.

*Safety is another problem. Many of these refugees are ex-soldiers from
the Vietnam war. You can find that many of them tear off the metal*

frames from the bunk beds to make spears to protect themselves from
other Vietnamese.

I have fun with Milton, trying to tease him into accepting our
cultural need for more specificity. "*Many* of them tear off the metal
frames? *How* many? Should I imagine fifty thousand former soldiers
armed with homemade spears? Or five hundred? Or fifty? Or five? If
you want to convince me, give me the details!"

"Oh, okay," he grins. "I don't really know how many."

We read on.

> *If they even make weapons at the refugee camps, what do you expect*
> *Hong Kong to do? As a result, the majority of the refugees are currently*
> *accommodated in closed or semi-open camps. In spite of this closed*
> *camp policy, you should know that open camps had once been used*
> *in the past. But problems like escape and Vietnamese committing*
> *robbery outside the camps were found. If you were living in Hong*
> *Kong, wouldn't you support the closed camp policy for these uniden-*
> *tified so-called Vietnamese refugees? Can you deny the fact that there*
> *may be other possible identities for these boat people?*

"No, I can't deny it. You won't *let* me deny it." I throw up my
hands in mock surrender.

Milton laughs. "So I should take out this last sentence?" he asks.

"Not necessarily," I tell him. "But in this context, questions like
these seem to underestimate the ability of the audience to make up
its own mind. What you're doing here is persuasion, rather than
academic argument. Persuasion is more like a speech, or advertising,
or an article by a columnist in a newspaper. Academic argument, at
least in the U.S., is supposed to appeal to the intellect rather than the
emotions. You're supposed to adopt a kind of cool, reasoned tone, and
assume that readers are going to make up their minds individually,
according to the evidence you present."[6]

Milton is not convinced about any of these style changes, but he is
so good-humored about it that it's hard to be exasperated with him.
On his next draft, he has added some citations, but he has just as
many questions—different ones, this time, but questions having the
same purpose and effect: persuasion rather than "argument" in the
academic sense. Milton is fully aware that he hasn't done what I
suggested; he even volunteers this particular paper for my research
because of his insistence on keeping the rhetorical questions, despite
my feedback. When I ask him why he has done so, he answers that
when he was writing, the questions just came to his mind naturally,
and so "I thought it would be fine to include them."

But a few weeks later, Milton, who is clearly enjoying thinking about his own style as well as my ideas about cultural difference, brings me a series of drafts of a paper about environmentalism in which he is trying to consciously keep track of his writing process and understand his audience. Speaking of global warming, he writes:

> In the meantime, you actually received some warnings and indications in the summer of 1988. How hot was it in the summer of 1988? Do you remember the news reporting the fact that it was the first time in history that U.S. farmers had not produced enough crops for Americans? Do you know that the world in 1988 suffered from the largest number of natural disasters within the decade? The failure of crop production in China, the prolonged drought in both Australia and India and the flooding in Ecuador and Peru are only part of the story of the disasters in 1988. Despite their seriousness, you may still forget or neglect all the evidence, but you should bear in mind that the global temperature only rose a single degree in 1988.

"Are these questions too aggressive?" Milton asks me.

"Yeah, maybe they are," I reply. We look at ways to mute the tone a little; I suggest changing the first sentence from the scolding "you" to "we," which to my mind makes it seem less accusatory, and changing some of the questions into statements to give the reader a greater sense of control. Looking at the changes he has made in the final draft, I can see that Milton has done a remarkable job keeping his own voice and his own style, while at the same time adjusting it to the needs of his new audience. When I tell him this, Milton thinks a minute and then replies good-naturedly, "Yes, I've always written for an audience, so why not now?"

Perhaps it is Milton's easygoing sense of humor, his adaptability and maturity that make it possible for him to take such a positive attitude. For others, it is more of a struggle, even with the same explanation of cultural differences. Yang Li, for example, the Taiwanese freshman who is doing an independent study with me to prepare himself for eventual admission to a U.S. law school, is, like Milton and Joseph, unconvinced of how seriously we take referencing others' ideas, or how much attention we pay to the conflicting opinions of various authors. Our meetings, which started with such promise—an uncommonly motivated student who is used to pushing himself to excellence, asking to spend time individually with me every week to talk about writing—have become somewhat tense as Yang Li finds one reason after another to avoid what he interprets as my criticism. When he chooses to argue noncontroversial issues, speaking in generalities about what "everybody believes," I explain why in this context he needs to choose an issue that is potentially divisive, examine several different opinions about it, and give at least a tentative, carefully reasoned opinion of his own. But Yang Li, who is young, and intense, and on his own for the first time, is resisting every suggestion I make. Our meetings soon become a polite battle of wills, with Yang Li forever finding evidence that the style he came with is already quite suitable in this new cultural context.

He never loses an opportunity, it seems, to discreetly point out to me the number of articles he has found that are written in the very style I am telling him is inappropriate here. *New York Times* editorials, for example, have no referencing, often have little direct discussion of the opposing view, do not weigh and balance differing opinions of authorities. The responses of U.S. military advisers, when asked by a *Harper's* reporter for their analysis of a proposal for armament reduction at the close of the Cold War,[7] are not studied, unemotional, evenhanded, carefully factual. "They're worse than me," says Yang Li, solemn-faced. He doesn't find this amusing; it is proof enough to him that I have been criticizing him for nothing. We look again at his paper on the environment.

> Consider our insatiable demand for paper products, which results in deforestation, the omnipresence of automobiles, which results in the emission of carbon dioxide, and the widespread use of refrigerators and air-conditioners, which results in the release of chlorofluoro carbons. We will then discover how deeply those environmentally hostile chemicals are rooted in our daily lives and, by extension, how each and every one of us are doing our delicate ecosystem a disservice each second around the world.

I explain again, as I have explained to him so many times, the need for either proof (of an "insatiable" demand for paper products) or for a muting of his language. Many people here will take you literally, I tell him. "Insatiable" means "unable to be satisfied." He nods. He knows the definition. "So if I had an insatiable demand for paper, I would be hoarding paper," I tell him, scooping some into a pile on my desk, "I would be running out to the supply cabinet to get more and more paper, because my need would be insatiable." Yang Li gives me a look of utter disgust. He isn't so naïve to imagine that anyone actually has an insatiable demand for paper. It's the effect that he wants to achieve, a shaming, coaxing, cajoling of his audience into line, prodding them into consensus and harmony.

Looking for ways to explain these differences to him, I pull out a file folder of issues of *Consider,* a free, weekly university publication consisting of two essays on opposing sides of a controversial issue. I ask Yang Li to pick a topic that interests him. He picks one on racism and begins to read the side of the page that argues that the civil rights movement has achieved nothing. I am reading the other side, a more positive piece that discusses the many problems that remain as well as the few advances made since the 1950s. I glance over at his side of the page and see that it has been written by a law student, using emotional language, speaking in generalities that he expects everyone to believe, or at least to accept, just because he said it so forcefully.

Yang Li, in his indirect, subtle way, has said nothing to me about this clear vindication of his view: that U.S. style is no different from his own. He simply sits and reads quietly, with intense concentration. I stop him, and ask him to read the other side of the page. Yes, we do have many forms of argument here, I tell him. Not everyone accepts the so-called academic form, the cool, rational, deliberate, carefully backed-up-with-evidence form that I am trying to get him to understand and accept as valid in this context. I tell Yang Li that I'd like him to try moving toward the type of argument advanced on the opposite page. I point out an assertion, and then a piece of support, right below it, then a concluding phrase. That is the form, in miniature, I tell him. Yang Li looks at me and says coolly, "For my next paper, I would like to do an argument that denies the existence of God."

I am startled, both at the change of subject and because I am not sure what to answer. This is a topic for philosophy, which seems to pull us away from the problems of providing factual evidence or dealing with the conflicting opinions of various authors, which are giving Yang Li so much trouble now.

"No," I decide, "you'd better stick with something current and controversial, something discussed in a national news magazine."

Yang Li nods. I assume the matter is settled.

The next week Yang Li arrives with a paper arguing against the existence of God. I look at the title page, incredulous, and then at Yang Li, who is laughing a little nervously.

"I feel frustrated," I say finally.

He nods.

"How do you feel?" I ask him.

"Frustrated," he says.

I laugh—too loud—and begin reading his paper.

The paper is good. In fact, it is damned good. It does a lot that we ask in academic argument: it looks carefully at the opposition, it presents a reply (albeit smug) to the opposition's arguments. It is smooth, logical, and sharp. But again, it has the subject all sewn up. No theologian could dispute it, according to this eighteen-year-old.

Facts and figures—careful, tangible evidence—are of course neatly avoided by the nature of the subject matter. And again, his references are carefully and correctly listed at the end of the paper, but are nowhere to be seen within the text.

I look up at Yang Li; he is waiting, nervous but defiant, for my verdict. I sense that we are at a standoff. I refuse to get angry, refuse to just tell him the paper is not acceptable because he didn't do the assignment. I want to get through to him, not just give orders. I'm just as stubborn as he is.

"I'll have to think about this, Yang Li," I tell him. "I'll get back to you in a few days." Whatever I decide, it will have to be quick. It's two weeks before the end of the semester, and he needs three drafts of everything, including the last assignment that he hasn't started yet. So far, he has given me only one draft of assignment one, three of assignment two, and one of assignment three, "The Existence of God."

At our next meeting I tell him what I have decided. It came to me early in the morning, as I was waking up, the time my head is clearest. I am pushing too hard. My response to frustration, an old habit. So I am going to take the pressure off. I sit back in my chair as I tell him this, making erasing motions with my hands.

"So. You're going to wash your hands of the whole thing," says Yang Li, with a bitter edge to his voice.

"No," I tell him. I am silent for a minute, thinking. "When we teach, sometimes we push, and sometimes we have to let up. This is a time I need to let up. It doesn't mean I care less."

Yang Li is sitting with his head bowed. "This is my most challenging class," he says.

There is no easy way to explain to students coming from collectivist backgrounds how they are expected to write, or think, or even to *be*, in this bizarre new context. A graduate student from Chile made me realize the implications of the paradigm shift we are asking them to make when she examined her own resistance to learning "a new way to write." "You said it was just a technique, but what I discovered was that it meant I had to look at things differently. Real differently. And in that sense, my world view has to change. You know, it's so powerful when you start to see things from a different perspective—the whole meaning of the world changes. So how am I going to change? Or would it make sense to me? All my life and everything is going to make sense in a different way. There is so much changing! And that's powerful. You see? I mean, that's incredible. That's so strong!"

4 "What Is Ancient Is Also Original"

The first time I taught academic writing to international graduate students, I was struck by their interest in clichés. I had put together a list of words and expressions that were prevalent in sloppy writing in our department, both in journal articles that were handed out to students and in students' attempts at sounding like the authors they read. "The current thrusts in our thinking," "in this era of knowledge explosion," "a total environment conducive to human growth and self-actualization"—such phrases were, in my opinion, either useless filler or painfully worn metaphors that had no place in good writing.

But instead of using the list to understand the kinds of tired platitudes to avoid, some of my students were carefully preserving them in their notebooks with translations in their own languages written neatly alongside. Some were even committing the list to memory. "We appreciate your handout on dead horses," they told me, laughing at the image. "We need this useful vocabulary."

At first I thought this meant I had underestimated my students' struggles with English. Some of them, I realized, had learned English only from textbooks and had had virtually no contact with native speakers before they arrived. During the first class sessions, these students were working with two dictionaries, looking up an unfamiliar English word in their own language and then back-translating with the second dictionary to make sure the meaning they had found was correct. Other students were much more at home in English because they had worked with Americans in international development agencies; others were English teachers or supervisors of English teachers at high levels. But because of their limited access to journals or books in their field—given the overcrowded, understocked libraries at some of their undergraduate institutions—the phrases that I considered mindlessly overused were perhaps completely new to them. For such students, a list of these expressions might have a certain value, I thought, as long as they realized that when they felt a little more at home at the U.S. university, they should begin to come up with words and ideas that were fresh and original.

But when I mentioned this to my friend Kamala, to share with her my amused embarrassment at an assignment that had backfired, she looked puzzled and was silent for some time. Finally she said, "I have a question about that word 'original.' " I was a little surprised, for I knew that Kamala had been speaking English for more than thirty years, first in her home country of Sri Lanka, then as a teacher in English-medium schools in eastern and southern Africa.

"Now I would say that what happened two thousand years ago was original and is still original," she began.

"What do you mean by that?"

"I mean there was an origin to it."

"Well sure, but . . ."

"And even after two thousand years, it is still original."

"How is that?"

Kamala hesitated. I could see that she wasn't just baiting me; she was really trying to understand something. I could feel her uncertainty and confusion, for she had often spoken of how mortified she felt when she didn't catch on to what her U.S. colleagues seemed to understand so easily. After all, she was a doctoral student. She had been speaking English all her life.

"When you say here that people are expected to use original terms, what do you mean?" she asked slowly. "That you have to create new . . . new things?"

"Yeah. You have to create new ways of putting words together."

"So it is: 'Create now.' "

"Yes. Create now."

"Mm hm," said Kamala, still trying to put it together. "What has been created in the past is no longer original."

"Right."

"So what has been created in the past, which is ancient, is no longer original."

Why does she keep repeating this? I wondered. Is this such a difficult idea? "Well, how do *you* see something ancient as still original?" I asked.

"I mean some ideas are not new. They're ancient. They still have the original meaning. They are still the original statement."

"Oh."

"They are original words. Original as they were created."

"Oh!" Again, the unsettling experience of looking into two worlds at the same time. "That's a different meaning of the word 'original.' "

Kamala nodded slowly, thinking.

"So if a professor tells you that you need to be more original," I began, remembering a comment she had made to me several months before.

"Yeah," she said, finishing my thought, "You see, back at home, if I said to my professor, 'This is original, this is what *I* mean,' it would have no value."

"It has to be—the *other* sense of 'original,' right?"

"Exactly," said Kamala. "You know," she said, laughing a little, "I'm glad that we got engaged in this discussion about the word 'original' because this is one of the things my professors keep telling me: 'You have to produce an original piece of work.' "

"And how were you interpreting that?"

"I guess I was trying to produce an original piece of work without understanding what was original to *him*. I mean, I know what is original to *me*. But when I brought that, he said,"—and here, Kamala took on a haughty, scolding tone, shaking her finger at me—" '*This* is not original. You can't keep reproducing what others have done!' "

"So you were interpreting the word 'original' as something that has been done before, and you had gone to the source . . . "

"Yes!" she said earnestly. "You have to search, you have to understand what has happened there, in that time, in that original work. So by simply learning it, it becomes original to you."

"Hm," I said, trying to imagine it.

"So that wasn't exactly satisfying to the professor," said Kamala, laughing as she remembered his bad mood that day, his frustration with her. He should have known better; he had worked with students from developing countries for nearly twenty years.

"And now, looking back on it, what do you think the professor really meant?" I asked.

"I think he meant I should have taken my own position!"

"Yeah," I agreed.

"But he didn't *say* that."

Both Kamala and the graduate students from China, Japan, India, Nepal, and Somalia who made up that first writing class come from societies that have for centuries valued the wisdom of the past over newness and individual creativity. These societies and, in fact, those of most of Asia, Africa, and the Middle East are still strongly influenced by religious and philosophical traditions that rest on assumptions about the nature of knowledge that are fundamentally different from those of the west. Wisdom, in the ancient traditions of most of the world, is not created—not socially constructed, not discovered through scientific experiment—but comprises great truths that have always existed and that can become known to people of enlightenment or superior wisdom. The traditional task of the student in such societies is to study various interpretations of these fundamental truths, to reflect on their meaning, and to apply them to their own lives and to society. This task is quite different from that of the western student, which is to formulate questions about something yet unknown, investigate those questions by gathering information from various sources, and put that information together in new ways to come up with something "original."

If I wanted to understand, in the academic tradition of the west, something about racism, for example, I would first need to think of a question I wanted to investigate such as "Is racism more of a problem on college campuses today than it was ten years ago?" I would then read some relevant studies to see what has already been "discovered" about this question, and then, if there were no such studies, or if I were dissatisfied with the way those studies had been carried out, I would think of a new way to investigate the problem: through certain interview questions, for example, or by reading key documents such as college mission statements or disciplinary codes. After I had collected my information, I would "analyze the data," that is, I would look for themes, or trends, or similarities and differences, in order to decide what conclusions I might draw that were relevant to my question. Finally, I would arrange my material in a style appropriate for my western academic audience—direct, to the point, explicitly connected, meticulously supported with evidence from the information I had collected in my study. This way of learning about racism would make sense to me if I assumed that knowledge can be created and challenged, even by a beginner, and that it can be seen as data to be manipulated, prioritized, discarded, or used in support of an idea that no one has had before.

But if I come from a tradition which assumes that knowledge is not gained by shuffling it around and breaking it into bits and reassembling it, but that it is there to be revealed to the thoughtful, reflective person who has the patience and discipline to study the interpretations of the past, I might not think it pertinent—at least in the context of a student-teacher or student-institution relationship—to ask questions about racism at all. I would instead seek to understand the timeless truths about human relations in general: how wise individuals have conducted themselves and have learned about the world; how the foolish have made common human errors, and so on. Through this general study, this slow progression from ignorance to understanding, I would eventually gain enough wisdom about race relations to act correctly in my own private life and to make decisions about racial difficulties in society. Whether college campuses have become more racist than they were ten years ago would, in a sense, be irrelevant; if everyone were to study, reflect, and apply timeless truths to their daily lives as they should, the problem would perhaps resolve itself.

"When a monk speaks to a problem," Kamala told me, "he doesn't analyze it in the western sense. He tells stories about Lord Buddha's life and then asks people to reflect upon their meaning for their own situation." She stood up then, and in a solemn voice as if she were reciting poetry, said:

> This is what happened
> This is how it happened
> These were the repercussions or consequences
> And this is how it was interpreted
> By this one
> By this one
> Or that one
> Or that one.

She sat down again and added, her eyes twinkling, "The monk doesn't say, 'Now please note: here, the results are "A," da da-da da-da, "B," da da-da da-da.' He won't say that. The effectiveness would be lost in our society. That elegance, that power of *holding* the audience and the respect it demands, would be lost."

These radically different approaches to understanding the world also rest on divergent assumptions about proper relations between teachers and learners, old and young, past masters and modern upstarts with new ideas. Societies that value the wisdom and authority of the past tend to be structured in hierarchies in which the social roles that people play are more important than individual personalities, and where respectful silence, rather than discussion and challenge, is characteristic of learning. These hierarchies are maintained by philosophical, religious, and social systems that are of course quite ancient; Confucianism, for example, has been the dominant force in China for two thousand years and was adopted by the Yi dynasty in Korea for half a millennium and by Tokugawa Japan for two hundred and fifty years, longer than the U.S. has existed (Yum 1991). In India, Hinduism stretches back three thousand years and teaches that the social order—relations between castes and classes as well as duties within the family—is neither derived from human reason nor imposed on people from the outside but "emanate[s] from the very nature and expression of reality at its deepest level" (Jain 1988, 80). And African societies, arguably the most ancient of all civilizations and the precursor of all that is "western" (Bernal 1987; UNESCO 1987), preserve through oral memory and teachings handed down through the generations an intricate hierarchy of social relations that encompasses not only the living but the dead and the yet unborn.

These traditions are not purely intellectual or theoretical, but permeate students' daily lives at every level, affecting the way they dress and carry themselves and cast their eyes in the presence of a superior, the language they choose, the tone of voice they adopt at different moments, the way they study and reflect and interpret events—even, as in Kamala's case, the meaning they ascribe to individual words. And all of these affect, in profound ways, how they write and think about writing. Kamala's assumption that what is ancient would be more valued by her professor than her own thoughts as a mere graduate student influenced her writing at every stage: the questions she chose to investigate, her research methods, the way she reported her data, even her tenaciousness in the face of her professor's criticism. And long after our conversation about the meaning of the word "original," even after she admitted that it made sense in the U.S. context to interpret it as "create now," she continued to think about research and writing the way she had long been taught: that one must repeat the wisdom of the past in order to understand the present.

Of course these two systems are not mutually exclusive, nor do they divide the earth neatly into east and west. World majority cultures have included western approaches to knowledge in their idea of education for a long time; formal education systems the world over are structured on French, British, American, or German models, and most students who come to a U.S. university have succeeded brilliantly in those systems. This is especially true in graduate schools, where students from "least developed countries" and ordinary backgrounds may be sent on scholarship funds from international development agencies. These students have had to fight their way through underfunded school systems that purposely fail the vast majority of students by the high school level. For example, in Togo, West Africa, a developing country of 3 million people with 75 percent of the population under age twenty and 1.5 million eligible for school, 13 percent of the grade 6 students passed the national examination in 1988. The tenth-grade exam weeded out 74 percent of those who remained. The passing grade is changed every year, depending on the education budget (Peace Corps 1988). Most of those who make it through high school have had a no-frills education. "We studied at night without electricity," a Togolese administrator for the Peace Corps told me. "We had to go out into the street to find a little light to read by. We copied all our books by hand—there were never enough to go around. I almost missed taking the high school examinations because I was helping my father work his fields up north. No one in my village had a radio, which was the only way to learn of our eligibility. Just by chance, a friend of the family happened to be passing through and told me I had to get to the city that day or I couldn't take the exam. I started out immediately on foot without a penny in my pocket or a bite of food in my stomach. No one in the village had any money they could give me. I walked for hours in the blazing sun, famished and unable to buy even a banana. When I finally made it to the first good-sized town, I managed to hitch a ride. Arriving at the exam site, I found that the examiners had been held up and couldn't make it until the following day. Fortunately, I found lodging with old friends, took the exam, and passed."

Students with such extraordinary determination to succeed in a western-based formal system have clearly been successful in taking on something of the western approach to knowledge as well as the mostly western subject matter. Nevertheless, these educational systems are set against a backdrop of the older intellectual traditions which permeate the family and community lives of both the students and their teachers. The result is that schools designed on western models are often taught by methods that are at least somewhat in keeping with the ancient traditions of the culture.

For many world majority students, knowing your place in the hierarchy and deferring to those of greater knowledge and to timeless, "original" wisdom have been part of life since childhood. Memory, in particular, plays such an important role in both ancient and modern varieties of education that in many cultures it is included in the definition of literacy. Children in China, for example, begin to develop their memory for the five thousand or so characters that are commonly used in writing[1] at the same age that U.S. children are mastering the twenty-six-letter alphabet. Even in Taiwan, influenced as it has been by western ideas and practices, most primary school teachers still require students to memorize their Chinese language lessons. In junior high school this practice continues; every lesson written in the old literary style is committed to memory. These kinds of lessons increase as students advance; in grade 7, the ancient style comprises about 30 percent of the texts, while in grade 9 it amounts to a good 60 percent (Liu 1986). So much is memory stressed that Liu, a Chinese psychologist, suggests that "one of the most conspicuous behavioral rules that Chinese children internalize is: 'If the purpose is to acquire the knowledge contained in an article, then the best strategy is to memorize the article' " (80).

Outside of the primary school system, children participate in other traditional forms of learning that further develop their memory, their patience, and their deference to wisdom and authority. In the Middle East, Africa, and Indonesia, children in Koranic schools learn to recite longer and longer passages of the holy book from memory, even though they may not understand the language, much less the content of what they are learning. A Somali doctoral candidate described his childhood experience in a Koranic school as an interesting sort of inside-out learning: first you memorized what you didn't understand, and only later, when you learned Arabic, did you gradually become enlightened as to the meaning of the words you held in your memory. In East Asian countries, traditional forms of learning are retained in the study of calligraphy, martial arts, flower arrangement, and painting; in China, students of calligraphy learn the five major styles by a rigidly prescribed series of steps—the same ones that have been used by calligraphy students for thousands of years—and may study for decades before they are allowed much deviation or originality. At the age when U.S. kindergartners are dripping and splattering paint with abandon, creating whatever forms and mixtures of colors come into their heads to give their creativity free rein, six-year-olds in China are copying classical examples of bamboo leaves and fish and roosters with a dexterity and perseverance that U.S. teachers rarely imagine lie within the capabilities of the young child. When these students reach the high school and college level and study the same modern disciplines taught in the west—computer science, chemistry, psychology, business management—their learning continues to be based more on "banking education," as Freire calls it (1986, 58), than on creativity and original thought—on the accumulation of facts rather than on the student's own analysis of what those facts mean or how to apply them to real-world problems. While teachers may be inspired lecturers or, in the earlier grades, master storytellers who hold the rapt attention of their students, teacher-student interaction in world majority cultures tends to rely—even more than it does in the U.S.—on factual question and answer rather than calling for students' opinions or encouraging dialogue. As classes are often overcrowded, students are generally not asked to do much writing, and what writing there is tends to be graded for correctness rather than original analysis.[2]

"Teachers in my country are not interested in your thoughts or how you are expressing things or analyzing things," a Somali graduate student told me. "They are looking at how you are using the language, the structure, the vocabulary, the grammar, things like that. But here you have to come up with your own ideas and express them and make arguments and analyze things, so that's a different level of difficulty, a different level of skill." "The value in education in our system is to have the information and to be able to give the information, not so much to manipulate the information," a Brazilian student adds. A Nepali student agrees: "In the schools at home, if you know more information, like the 'Seven Wonders of the World' kind of thing, you are regarded as knowledgeable or learned. It's more of a top-down system. The teacher comes and dumps all the information into the student's head, and the student would receive that and be happy with it." Along with this emphasis on correct information comes an unusually deferential attitude—from the U.S. point of view—toward the "knowers" of that information: those who in ancient times would have mastered the entire body of knowledge orally and who now, by virtue of their advanced degrees, are still quite venerated. "In my country, the professor is in the balcony, and we are down here," a Sri Lankan student told me. "We believe that if you're a professor you know everything in the world. Here, in one of my first classes, the professor asked me, 'Do you think this is correct?' And he really didn't know the answer. I was shocked. Oh my God, in our culture a professor will never ask a student, 'Do you think? Is it that? I just can't remember, I don't know that area.' In my culture the professors never say they don't know. Or if they really don't know, they might give some evasive answer just to keep the students' respect."

So important are the teachers' words that newcomers to the U.S. system may, on occasion, have difficulty with the idea of manipulating them at all. A graduate student from the Philippines came into my office one day with a paper on third world economics, saying he was having trouble with transitions. His TA had apparently been working with him but had not been successful in helping him stitch the unconnected parts of his paper together. It was a puzzling paper, for in many places the text flowed smoothly and understandably, but suddenly it would jump to a completely unrelated topic and then begin to flow as smoothly as before. As I talked with the student about how he had put his paper together, it became clear to me that he had been trying to preserve his professor's words by taking whole blocks of his lecture notes and trying to rearrange them in a way that would somehow respond to an assignment to develop his own thesis. Since the student had no thesis—at least no thesis he was willing to state in his paper—his strategy wasn't working, but the reasons for attempting to write this way were perfectly logical from his point of view, for if he succeeded, he would have a paper that was "original" in Kamala's sense of the word, a paper that went to the source, the original words, the original statement, of the professor.

It would be hard to imagine a U.S. student approaching an assignment in quite this way; here, beginning writers are more likely to produce papers based solely on their own opinions without any authority at all to back them up. Rather than venerating the past, many of my U.S. freshmen find even recent history boring or naïve and have difficulty imagining my experience with school segregation in the 1950s, or political protest in the 1960s, or even TV shows in the 1970s. Indeed, Margaret Mead (1970) has pointed out that the children of the 1960s were the first generation whose lives were so different from those of their parents that the old had to learn from the young rather than the other way around. Though she saw this change from "postfigurative cultures" of the past to "prefigurative" ones of the future as a worldwide trend, nowhere is it more apparent than in the U.S., where an innovative scientific climate and a fiercely competitive capitalism create the expectation that "newness" will be part of any curriculum, any product, any idea worth mentioning, because it is so closely connected with our ideas of intelligence and success.

U.S. "mainstream" students, then, are not surprised by their professors' expectations that they "create new things" and that they plunge right into the battle of conflicting opinions and ideas—the academic "conversation"—in their disciplines. Though some hesitate to do this or may grow to question the value of it, in general they are somewhat more inclined than students from more hierarchal or collectivist cultures to take on this voice and persona, both because of the emphasis our culture places on newness and because of our egalitarian assumptions, our conviction that equality among individuals is "self-evident." For if students are to criticize someone else's ideas, they must be able to think of themselves, potentially at least, on the level of the authorities themselves.

True egalitarianism in social and professional life in the U.S. is a "polite fiction,"[3] of course. Everyone knows that differences in power, status, and wisdom do exist; nevertheless, our dress, our body language, our informal protocol even in formal situations, all maintain the fiction that we are all "just folks." To world majority students who have been raised to be comfortable with a certain degree of hierarchy, our efforts to act as though status differences do not exist can be both amusing and faintly embarrassing. "I am the director of the English Language Institute and a tenured professor in linguistics," a friend of mine announced to a group of nervous new Asian undergraduates, "and I have worn a jacket and tie for your benefit. Normally you will find me in jeans and a sweatshirt." The students laughed, as he expected, and the ice was broken. In my own department the director sits at the head of the table in staff meetings, to be sure, but he, too, wears jeans, pours his own coffee, keeps his door open, and expects to be called by his first name. References to his decision-making power are kept veiled by faculty; they would be an embarrassment to him if mentioned in his presence. In my classes, I affect a similar fiction with the U.S. graduate students I am training to teach writing in the disciplines; I am the "facilitator" of their discussion rather than a lecturer, and I claim to know something about teaching writing, but I also readily admit that I know next to nothing about their fields of expertise: art history, economics, Russian cinema, electrical engineering. We meet at noon to eat lunch together and talk in a friendly fashion about how to design assignments, or come up with assessment criteria, or respond to student papers; I take attendance quietly and unobtrusively, as if I had no power to declare their participation inadequate, an act which would cost them their teaching assistantships and thus their graduate school tuition waivers and medical benefits. My discomfort with power over my adult students and my teaching philosophy that consciously aims to reduce the power distance between us have been influenced by—even created by—my upbringing in a society that holds egalitarianism as an ideal.

This cultural emphasis on equality creates an expectation of "critical analysis" or, at least, off-the-top critique, a task my U.S. graduate students take to with relish. I asked them one day to give me their reaction to some assignments written by professors in various disciplines. After showing them some obviously poor ones, I suggested they look at one I thought was pretty good, a history assignment that addressed skills that many undergraduates have trouble with: writing a concise summary of several articles, then analyzing another author's critique of those articles, and finally giving their own reasoned opinion of them.

"What's your reaction to this assignment?" I ask them.

"Yech," says the economics TA.

"What do you mean, yech?"

"This assignment leaves absolutely no room for the students' own ideas," he says. "Look here, the professor is just telling them to summarize the articles, and then chronicle what other authors have said about them."

"That's right," nods the art history TA. "Even though the assignment says they're supposed to add their own opinion, it's just tacked onto the end of the paper as an afterthought. With all the emphasis these days on the quality of undergraduate education, it's incredible that instructors are still assigning stuff like this!"

But graduate students coming from societies that are not based on this assumption of equality tell me that they must often stifle the critical thoughts and ideas that arise in their minds as they sit respectfully listening to the teachings of past masters or the maxims of present-day ideologies. A Mainland Chinese student told me, "In China, we don't usually speak out our own opinion, even in an academic discussion. An idea will flash in your mind, but if you want to give a new idea, you need to think carefully and be well prepared, because teachers and old people don't like young people to criticize. If you give a new idea it might be negative to old ideas, and they are fond of old ideas."

A Japanese student who had been in a U.S. graduate program for several years added, "I used to feel guilty in Japan because I was too critical. In Japan, the teacher teaches, the students take notes. The better you learn what the teacher says, the better student you are. As soon as you ask an interesting question, it's rude. Can you be that smart, to carry on an academic discussion with a teacher? And then there's the peer pressure. Questioning authority will cause ostracism. The Japanese are so eager to create harmony. You just can't break the harmony."

But despite the emphasis on harmony, memorization, and top-down teaching methods, these students are not so beaten down by the system as some might expect. The graduate students I talked to were quick to point out many ways in which questioning and debate are valued outside of their admittedly rigid school systems. "In your country," a Somali told me, "politics is just a matter for politicians. But down there, everybody is a politician." Because of the clash of the old and the new, he told me, there are constant debates going on: the efficiency of cost-effective government versus the security of the older patronage system, the effect of changing values on young people, the possible outcomes of increasing liberalization of religious views. "Everyone hears these debates going on, and everyone argues with friends and colleagues about them," he told me. "We may have to keep our opinions to ourselves at school, but after school is a different story."

"When you live in a country where inflation is 2,000 percent a year," adds a Brazilian student, "you know that every day things are changing. You don't know if next month you're going to wake up and have the same president as you did last month or if when you go out you're going to come back alive. If you are living in a system where nothing stays the same, you have to be very flexible in your thinking."

Thus, regardless of the respect for tradition that students are expected to exhibit both within the formal school system and in the extracurricular forms of education that surround it, many world majority students do have the opportunity, even the necessity, of active, intense debate. Of course these opportunities are given more to men than to women; women graduate students from Indonesia, Sri Lanka, Chile, and Korea all told me similar stories of being silenced, in their own cultures, by the expectation that it was proper for a woman to keep her ideas to herself.

"My brain is working, but not expressing," said an Indonesian woman, who, after a year in a U.S. master's program, was still struggling to speak up in class. "Maybe my personality has become conditioned to this situation. In my work at home, most of the employees are men who are more powerful than us, so they tend to talk a lot and influence us. So instead of saying no, we say yes." Under pressure to speak up in the U.S. academic environment, this student sometimes continues to say the opposite of what she really thinks. "I want to say, for example, that I like the way this author wrote. But instead of starting with 'I like,' I start with other words, for example, 'I don't like.' So if I say 'I don't like,' it means I should change the whole idea in my mind. And when I change my words, it doesn't have any relation with what is really in my mind. And when it comes out differently, people react differently, too, based on what I'm saying. And after that I feel, wow, I shouldn't say that. It's awful. I feel like it's just, you know, rubbish."

These cultural and gender expectations directly affect not only the students' class participation, but the way they think about and organize their writing. A Sri Lankan student, for example, linked her difficulty giving her own opinion in her papers with the demeanor she had been expected to adopt in professional meetings in her own country. "You have to be so modest," she told me. "If you are eager, it's considered uncultured. You have to know the tricks of the trade. The most important person at the meeting is not going to talk at the beginning. It's the less important officers who will start. The most important things come up late. So you have to know how to restrain yourself. You have to look for cues from your director that now is the time to speak. It's very hierarchical. We have to know our place." This lifelong habit of restraint, she told me, has made it nearly impossible for her to make her own ideas prominent in her writing, even in her doctoral dissertation.

A Korean graduate student told me that the difficulty she had with repeating herself in class as well as in her papers came from never being expected to say much about the ideas she had always had in her mind. "I didn't have the chance to be trained to speak publicly," she said, "so when I speak in class I always feel I'm under pressure and that no one is going to listen to me. So I have to say what I want to say very fast, and then I kind of get lost in my mind, kind of mumbling a lot. I say stupid things, or the same things over and over." This experience has made her writing sound "illogical," she says, and gives her particular difficulty with transition words, which signal a western writer's strong, direct movement through the argument.

This reticence to speak out, this "mumbling" or silence from many of the women and the preference for received knowledge on the part of both women and men from world majority cultures should not be misinterpreted to mean that these students necessarily suffer from a lack of confidence in themselves or in their own ideas. In the west, where individuality, originality, and egalitarianism are cultural ideals, a person is assumed to be "mature" when these traits are developed to the fullest. While this assumption makes a certain amount of sense in a western cultural context, it cannot be generalized to explain human development the world over. Unfortunately, researchers commonly make this mistake, and their resulting studies, which so confidently lump together people coming from very different social and intellectual traditions, add to our difficulties in trying to step outside the set of values and assumptions that we consider "normal and natural."

For example, *Women's Ways of Knowing,* a widely read text in women's studies, chronicles the development of thinking in women from a variety of ethnic backgrounds toward a "secure, integrated and enduring self-concept" (Belenky et al. 1986, 81). In the view of the authors, women who are silent "have only begun to think about thinking" (23) and represent "an extreme in denial of self and in dependence on external authority for direction" (24). In their silence, the authors contend, these women "do not cultivate their capacities for representational thought." Citing Luria's studies of Russian peasants who, Luria claimed, had not developed the capacity for abstract thinking, the authors draw a parallel between peasants leading a "medieval way of life" (26) and the silent women they interviewed in the U.S., who mostly come from "socially, economically and educationally deprived" backgrounds (23) and grew up "in great isolation" from their peers (32). Though the authors draw a distinction between these lonely, abused women and the Russian peasants, who came from communities with rich interpersonal connections and who had a "sense of we-ness with others" (27), they suggest that both groups lack the ability to think abstractly because "they do not explore the power that words have for either expressing or developing thought" (25).

But as world majority women point out, in other cultural contexts women's silence can be a position of power, one that creates a space for internal dialogue and reflection rather than weakness and stupidity. *"I resisted having to submit to a particular area of life just because I was female,"* Kamala wrote in a paper called "How Did I Come To Know?"

> *I was silent at times, but my silence was followed by action. I would do things to provoke other family members into speaking. In my silence I wanted to find out how it would be wrong if I did differently what was expected of me. I was silent not because I was afraid to be noisy, but because I needed space and time to make meaning of what they said, so that I would be prepared for my next move. I was silent because I wanted the space and time to cherish my sense of accomplishment.*

"Silence in my culture is the base for thinking," she added. "In the U.S. I've noticed that people are very nervous if there is silence for one second. You must fill the silence; you must start talking quickly. That seems a little immature to me."

Women who are more comfortable with received knowledge than original thought fare little better in *Women's Ways of Knowing;* whether they come from U.S. mainstream culture or from abroad (40), "received knowers" feel confused and incapable when the teacher requires that they do original work. "They don't really try to understand the idea," the authors lament. "They have no notion, really, of understanding as a process taking place over time and demanding the exercise of reason. They do not evaluate the idea. They collect facts but do not develop opinions" (42). Received knowledge, the authors claim, is "clearly maladaptive for meeting the requirements of a complex, rapidly changing, pluralistic, egalitarian society," so women need to be stimulated to develop "more adequate conceptions of knowing" (43). It is even intimated that received knowing is a childish position; the authors point, perhaps somewhat ironically, to male authorities (Kohlberg, Piaget, and Erikson) whose studies purport to show that the "shift in orientation . . . from external authority, which binds and directs our lives, to an adherence to the authority within us, is one of the central tasks of adolescence" (54).

This analysis and others that ignore or gloss over the cultural assumptions upon which they are based reinforce the assumption that, as liberal or progressive educators, we think we have moved beyond the old simplistic idea that western culture represents the pinnacle of civilization not only technologically but cognitively. This form of self-congratulation in turn makes it all the more difficult to see the possibility of other routes to wisdom, other intelligent ideas of evidence, other valid ways of exploring the limits of human potential, other methods of learning and teaching.

Given the abundance of studies of human development that continue to consider the world from a single point of view, it is gratifying to come across other researchers who are open enough to other cultures to doubt their original assumptions. For instance, Howard Gardner, a Harvard psychologist who has been studying creativity for two decades, confessed that after four visits to Mainland China he was "overcome with a welter of impressions, feelings, questions, conclusions. Some of my most entrenched beliefs about education and human development had been challenged by my observations in Chinese classrooms," he wrote, and this feeling of "culture shock," of being "alternatively mesmerized and repelled" by what he saw there, caused him to sit down and, "in a frenzy more characteristic of Georges Simenon than a sober psychologist," draft in less than two weeks a book challenging his own views of progressive education (Gardner 1989, preface).

While he had originally been convinced that creativity must be nurtured early in a child's life and would be thwarted by an early emphasis on memorization and imitation, Gardner saw in China that children who were taught ink and brush painting by traditional methods and were allowed no opportunities for creative expression in school were nevertheless able to use their skills to "adapt their schemas to new challenges." He recounts how he gave a class of six-year-olds an assignment to draw a gadget they had never seen before—his son's collapsible baby stroller. Although the children had never drawn an object without first being instructed in the correct way of doing it, they took to the task with great interest and energy, Gardner says, and, to his surprise, produced drawings similar to those that might be drawn by "highly competent six-year-old western children" (1989, 245) who had been encouraged to exercise creativity during their preschool years. This experience and others in China led him to the realization that, although the Chinese education system "embraces 'mimetic' modes in the most rigorous (and often rigid) way imaginable," this type of teaching does not turn students into puppets who can only repeat what their teachers have taught them. And although the Chinese have traditionally learned in silence, through received knowledge, this has "not prevented their culture from making the most remarkable technological and aesthetic discoveries over the millennia" (15).

Despite these hopeful signs that western researchers are becoming more open to the validity of other approaches to learning, many in the U.S. university system remain sadly isolated by their assumptions of superiority of the western view. When I asked the professor who had given Kamala so much trouble about "originality" why he thought some "non western" students had difficulty writing analytical papers, he told me, "Our culture believes in the value of thinking and the value of self-expression. It's a very cultural thing. But some students don't know what analysis is; it is totally foreign to them. It's something that's been explicitly trained out of them. Their school system has taught them 'Thou shalt not think, thou shalt not speak, thou shalt repeat.' They've had the curiosity beaten out of them." Faced with Kamala's continued insistence on repeating old knowledge rather than creating new, her professor assumed that she and other students who had learned to appreciate rather than critique, to grasp knowledge as a whole, and to find wisdom in what is ancient rather than in their own novel ideas had been victimized by their educational and cultural systems because they continued, in the western university, to approach knowledge the way they had been so carefully and thoroughly taught.

Thus, when Magdalena, a first-year Puerto Rican student in my class in academic argument who had been at the top of her class in a private, English-medium high school in her country, is confronted with her first assignment in the U.S.—to put together an argument based on her own opinion—she stitches together unreferenced, barely altered quotations from five sources so skillfully that I do not realize, until I am halfway down page two, that the words are not her own. And when Jean-Claude, a reflective, highly articulate graduate student from Côte d'Ivoire, fails to produce a comprehensible master's thesis, he confesses that his method of gathering facts on note cards is to thumb through books picking out quotes to "ornament the text," rarely reading anything at all, with the result that the quotes bear little relation to the ideas he is trying to present.

It is not surprising that these students are using quotes to "sound intelligent" or to "make the paper look good"—this is common enough with struggling writers from any culture. What is more telling is their polite but decided skepticism when I advise them to quote authorities not just for the sake of authority but to add weight to their own arguments. Jean-Claude, for example, had been so involved with the task of choosing and quoting what other authors said that he was not even really aware that their words made no sense the way he had arranged them until I asked him to read his text aloud and explain to me what it meant. It was then we discovered that the reason he didn't know how the quotes related to his argument was that he was not fully convinced they were *supposed* to relate to his argument. Like the graduate student from the Philippines who tried simply to rearrange his lecture notes in order to preserve the professor's original words and ideas, Jean-Claude assumed that the purpose of citation is to demonstrate knowledge of what authorities said in as close to their own words as possible rather than critiquing them or using them to add weight to his own original thesis.

This quoting of authorities for authority's sake, so common in world majority cultures, is reinforced by the French system of education in many of its former colonies. Not only does the inherent racism of colonialism accentuate the idea of teacher-as-authority in the classroom, but the French system of education in France is itself quite authority-bound. In a well-known cross-cultural study of IBM managers in various cultures, "power distance"—a measure of a culture's acceptance of hierarchical relations—was found to be higher in France than in any other European country, higher even than in some world majority cultures (El Salvador, Turkey, East Africa, Thailand, Iran, and Japan).[4] A U.S. professor of international management told me that he had spent a sabbatical year in France taking university business courses because he thought it would be interesting to get the European perspective. "I couldn't get over the extent to which the students were stenographers," he told me. "The lecture was given; the man read from—the *Man* read from the *Book!* Then he'd look up and paraphrase what he had just said. His whole delivery was based on this. And the students dutifully wrote down what it was they were supposed to learn."

U.S. students, too, may be compulsive note takers at times and may have trouble critiquing and manipulating the words of the authors they read, but this difficulty seems to come more from a confusion about how to build a complex argument than from difficulty with the *idea* of questioning authority within the formal school system or with using the words of authorities to their own ends. And while a U.S. student may be afraid to challenge the TA's pet theory for fear of getting a poor grade on a paper, or may be very tentative in advancing ideas, keeping them vague or hidden out of a lack of confidence as an academic writer, the student probably has no real reluctance, in a comfortable classroom setting, to disagree with authors on the reading list or to contribute independent ideas to the discussion because the student has been raised to think—and in fact will tell us at every opportunity—that everyone has a right to their own opinion. U.S. students may thus be able to catch on to the idea of "academic argument" or "critical thinking" more quickly than some students coming from systems that value the authority of the past not because of superior intellect or a higher quality secondary education, but because their minds and the educational system that fostered them have been shaped by the assumptions of their culture.

So too have world majority students been shaped by the assumptions and values of the long-established traditions they have grown up with. Despite the westernizing trends that have touched so many countries worldwide—the increasing availability of western goods, the influence of the U.S. and European media, the growing sense of individualism associated with these new freedoms and choices—the ancient assumptions still underlie the decisions many world majority students make about writing. But at the same time, when they understand what it is that we expect of them, when they are convinced that questioning, critique, and creative originality are what we are looking for, they may take to the new task with surprising vigor.

Jieming, a Mainland Chinese student who has two undergraduate degrees and a master's in psychology from Beijing universities and who is now doing a master's in psychology in the west, has rarely written a paper in which her own opinion was called for. Although she has great difficulty with English and does not consider herself much of a writer in her own language, something in the classroom atmosphere, perhaps the possibility of putting on paper the ideas that had been out of the question in China, drove her to work three times as hard as most of my other students just to bring the words under control.

> On April 15, 1989, Hu Yao-bang, the former Secretary of the Chinese Communist Party, died of heart disease in Beijing. His death became a blasting fuse that resulted in a great democratic movement in China. College students and young teachers were the pioneers of this movement, which rapidly expanded from campuses to the whole society, from Beijing to other big cities, with millions of people involved in it. As everyone knows, the democratic movement has been put down by military force. The cruel slaughter gave a horrid shock to all the people in the world. Many experts on China tried to figure out the cause of the movement, and many thought it was incredible that the Chinese government could use such cruel means to deal with a non-violent movement. But looking back at Chinese history, one may believe that what had happened was a reappearance of certain historical trends. . . .

Jieming did not always do the assignments or follow the conventions for academic writing that we talked about in class, preferring to write what she seemed to need at the moment. She would typically hand in papers late, breathless and disheveled, with a thousand apologies and an expression of pure triumph. Her note to me at the end of her paper on the events in Tiananmen Square is a poignant expression of the contradictions so many world majority students bring to western classrooms: the combination of deference to authorities—both to teachers and to the general wisdom of texts—and the power of the creative, analytical mind to shake free of constraints when given the invitation to do so:

> *Note: I have read some books and articles on the democratic movement that happened in China in 1989. But it is hard for me to say from which resources I have drawn any ideas to put into this paper. However, one thing is clear; that all the knowledge and the ways I used to think and write are what I have learned from my teachers and others, although I have used my own mind to absorb and integrate them. I am very grateful to those who gave me knowledge and let me know how to recognize the world. And I am also very sorry that I did not put any references at the end of this paper.*

5 Something Inside Is Saying No

"You know, Helen, the comment I get so often from professors is that I need to be improved. And I don't really agree with that. I have a real problem with that. I say, what improvement, in what context? What does improvement imply?"

Surya and I were in the tiny kitchen of a friend's apartment getting ready for a Center party—predictably, a potluck of dishes from a dozen cultures. I was chopping green chilies for a curry, and Surya was standing at the sink, filling a huge rice pot with water.

"I don't need to improve myself in order to write because I've been writing for a long time," said Surya, turning off the faucet and wiping his hands delicately on a dish towel. "I'm a professional. I can write, nicely."

I glanced his way. His face was flushed with unusual emotion, though he was still smiling his perpetual smile. "Come to Nepal, you will see my articles in the newspaper, you will see my book. What do you mean by improvement?"

I raised an eyebrow in surprise. Although Surya had taken my graduate writing class two years ago and had been in several classes with me as a fellow student, this was the first time I'd heard he was a published writer. When he was recommended to me as a potential student, professors simply said that he had writing problems and would probably benefit from my class.

"Wow, Surya, I've never heard you talk like this!" In fact, I had never heard Surya speak negatively of anything or anyone in the three years I had known him. Excessively polite, even obsequious both in speaking and in writing, he was prone to hyperbole, massive over-generalization, and beating around the bush, all of which had caused him trouble in his academic papers. As his instructor, I had talked with him about the need to be more plain-spoken; phrases like "I was dying to be engulfed in their politeness" would not help him to be taken seriously, I thought, in an academic context. Surya had laughed a little at this, and he agreed to tone down his language and to make an attempt to adopt a more straightforward style. But now, on hearing that I was going around with a tape recorder interviewing students about their frustrations with writing at the U.S. university, Surya had begun to hint, ominously, that he had something he wanted to say to our whole department before he left for home. "Frustrations? You want frustrations?" he would say on meeting me in the hallway. "Have I got something for you!"

A group of students came into the kitchen carrying dishes full of potluck—chicken with peanut sauce, tabouli piled high on lettuce leaves, chips and hot salsa, brownies, lemon pie. There were greetings all around, and a hunt for a larger table. Kamala came in with a couple of shopping bags, sniffed, and nodded approvingly at the spices I was stirring in the hot oil. Someone turned on the music in the next room, a cheerful West African shuffle. More bodies pressed into the kitchen. Surya poured a pitcher of rice into the pot of boiling water and took over the stirring of the curry from Kamala. "We'll talk later," he assured me, smiling. "Have I got something for you!"

A few days later, we settled ourselves in a corner of the library and turned on the tape recorder. "So tell me about those frustrations," I said warmly. "Tell me about the problems you've had with people wanting to improve your writing, or with the process you went through to try to change your style."

But Surya responded to my direct questions with polite confusion, laughing a little, claiming that he didn't really know what I meant, that he didn't really know what to say. "Let me talk about how I feel about writing," he said finally. "Let me tell you about writing in my own language, Nepali." And so I listened while he told me the story the way he wanted to—beginning with how he had learned to write as an adolescent and working his way through his university career to his job with the Ministry of Education, adding many factual details about Nepali culture that he felt I needed to know. Only after he had established the context in this way did he let himself slip back into the indignant mood he had felt at the party and get to the heart of what he wanted to say.

I realized only later, on reading the written transcripts of the interviews, how similar Surya's oral style was to the way he organized some of his class papers. As he told me during the interview, "In our [Nepali] writing style, no matter what kind of writing it is, we would not write in such a way that you would see the whole point in one paragraph or one page. We would come up with a lot of background information which would be considered redundant here in this context. For example, if someone asked me to write about a theory in economics, I would be tempted to write the history of how that theory evolved and who are the people that contributed to the theory. So that would set the context. And then I would go into describing what that theory is all about. . . . And then I would analyze based on that context—looking at a particular problem in the light of existing circumstances of the context, how that is affecting others and whether or not we can compare it with other systems or other problems. And then from there I can draw a solution to that problem. . . . So that's my style, and that is pretty much accepted in our academic writing."

But Surya had not learned to write in school. Although he had a master's degree in economics from a Nepali university, he had never written long papers; his progress had always been assessed by multiple-choice or short-answer exams. Instead, he had learned by writing under the guidance of family members, for real audiences and for purposes that were immediately discernible and practical. This interested me, because my own development as a writer had followed much the same course; I too had never written much more than short-answer exams in high school or college, but had learned to take writing seriously by watching my mother, who would stay up late at night chain-smoking and pounding out her family history on an old manual typewriter. She would give me her drafts sometimes and ask my opinion of them, and together we would get down on our hands and knees on the living room floor and cut and paste—literally—on the threadbare rug. And then, when I went away to university, she would write me letters, more than I could hope to return, and I would write back, trying to explain the new ideas I was learning in subjects that I had never imagined existed, arguing with her over Freudian theory or new findings in cultural anthropology. By the time I began to write for publication I had written hundreds, even thousands of letters: letters home from abroad; multipaged Christmas cards, different for each recipient; letters to newspapers and product manufacturers and political figures. When an editor suggested I turn one of my letters into an essay, I had to go to the library and read Montaigne and E. B. White before I was confident that I knew what an "essay" was. But even though I'd had no formal training in writing and had rarely received feedback from an instructor, I was able to succeed to a certain extent as an essayist by writing naturally about what I had been thinking about, much the way I had always done.

Surya, too, had learned to write at home, in the ways he naturally expressed himself and that writers in his culture found appropriate. First of all, he told me, he had been influenced by a brother fifteen years his senior who had been a journalist for Nepal's national newspaper. "Because of our age difference, he treated me like his own son. He was wonderful to me, and I really admired him. So I developed the habit of writing at home." Surya's eye for detail and sense of audience had continued to grow under the influence of his father, who would call him into his room and question him whenever Surya came home from an excursion outside Kathmandu valley. "'What are the people doing over there?' he would ask. 'Are they different from us?' He was so very eager to know all these kinds of things. And after hearing from me he would comment to his friends, 'Oh look, my son went to that village and he found that people do these things differently.' He was a real communicator in the community. And just to please him I would collect information, I would try to learn as much as I could and observe the cultural differences very carefully so I could present them to him."

As Surya developed his writing, he began to incorporate into it the formal Sanskrit vocabulary of the Hindu classics. "My parents expected us to read holy books to them at night—the *Ramayana*, the *Bhagavad Gita*. And so I was very much influenced by this experience, because we think that if you can use Sanskrit vocabulary in your writing, it will be just superb! And so I must tell you that my vocabulary is very good by Nepali standards."

However, Surya soon discovered that regardless of how much his vocabulary was admired, this elegant literary style was not suited to every occasion. When he took his first job, as a coordinator for a literacy program, his duties included writing short books and pamphlets for adults who had just learned to read. "At that point I had to change my style completely," said Surya, "because the common people didn't understand those big Sanskrit words. It was hard at first, to write in this new style, but I went out into the villages and listened to the people and learned to use their vocabulary, which was really different. And then when I got into my field of nonformal education I began to do technical writing in English, the language of the foreign donor agencies. I had to compare programs, and write reports and evaluations, and prepare proposals. So I got used to writing for different audiences and purposes. And at the same time, I was publishing short expressive pieces in the newspaper in a very personal style, the style I like best. When I express my feelings, especially in Nepali, my writing flows, it flows just like a river." Surya laughed, a little self-deprecating laugh that politely covered his pride. "I can write, Helen. It may not seem so here, but I am a writer."

As soon as Surya arrived at the U.S. university, he began getting feedback from his professors that startled him, both in its direct, matter-of-fact tone and in its content. My own comment on a personal experience piece he did for my class—one of the first classes I taught for international graduate students—was the following:

> Surya—Your vocabulary is excellent—maybe even too excellent. "I was dying to be engulfed in their politeness" sounds so overdone as not to be plausible. Another problem here is that the point of your story is too subtle for Americans (or *me*) to catch. I'm not sure why America was to you the land of politeness. I'm a bit confused about what you did wrong in the airport line. And finally, I'm not sure of your conclusion. . . .

"The hardest comments I got—and that I still get—are that I must be more direct," Surya told me. "But in Nepal, if someone is direct, everybody says he is not a good writer. Here, I am supposed to be very aggressive, both in my vocabulary and in my style. I am supposed to do what you call critical analysis. But in Nepal, our style of analysis is different, because people feel pretty much bad about criticizing others. Let me give you an illustration. If you have a party at your house and you forget to invite someone, you are not going to see that person again. People are that much sensitive! Even if you remember just before the party and call him and say, 'I'm sorry I didn't invite you sooner, but could you come?' And he would say, 'It's all right, I know you are busy, you forgot, never mind.' But he would never show up. So that kind of thing is reflected in our writing. That sensitivity."

"In Nepal, we never criticize except in a very indirect way. Instead of telling you directly, I might talk about another person who had the same experience as you. I would say, 'Let me tell you this story, let me tell you the kind of problems my friend had, and here is the solution that person found in the end.' So in that way you can see what I am suggesting. Even a teacher will criticize in a very indirect way! If he thinks I need some improvement or that my point is off the track, he might say, 'Well, the way you are doing it is nice, that is one way to look at it, but now you are living in a different context. So now how would you do it if you were in that context?' He would never say, 'Well, your writing is absolutely off the point.' "[1]

But at that time, Surya's instructors—including myself—did not understand the connection between culture and "good writing." Hyperbole was hyperbole in our book. If the point of your paper will not come clear after repeated tries, you've got a writing problem. And Surya's reluctance to wrestle with ideas of different authors was even more problematic. Nobody wanted to suggest openly that it might be a deficit in intellectual preparation, a "thinking problem." Cultural difference had too often in the past been linked with cultural deficit, and the last thing we wanted to do was to perpetuate the idea that cognitive abilities in one culture are superior to those in another. Nevertheless, the uncomfortable realization in our department was that "non western" students seemed to have somewhat more trouble with "analysis," on average, than U.S. students. And so, not knowing that Surya was already an accomplished writer, we chalked it up to his lack of experience in writing long papers at school and told him that his writing would improve with practice.

Though Surya was insulted by our advice, he did not show it. "Because of my cultural background, I would never confront anyone about the comments they made about my writing," he told me. "Besides, I had to succeed so I wouldn't lose face with my family back home. That's what all international students have to put up with, the terrible importance their families put on success. But in order to succeed, I would have to change. I would have to learn to use a very aggressive style that would more or less—you know—slap the reader in the face. My God, that was really hard. You cannot change your habits of a lifetime overnight. Imagine, a person who comes from that kind of culture, who spends half his life, thirty years, forty years, writing, working with people, and then they come here for one or two years, do you expect him to be able to change his style?

"Can he?" I asked.

"Ah, to some extent," Surya answered, smiling. "He can learn new vocabulary. He can force himself to adopt the direct type of organization. But doing this would be very painful, and at the end he would not feel satisfied. It might turn out to be an excellent paper in this system, but to him it would be nothing."

"And so," he continued, "I began to lose confidence. I began to feel, 'Gee, Surya, you're stupid.' And you know, 'You can't write.' That voice was coming from here, from this culture. But at the same time another voice which was with me was saying, 'Surya, don't worry, you're all right, don't lose your confidence, you can do fine, just try to learn the ideas, you don't have to concentrate on the language or the writing style.' And really, sometimes it got very tense between the two voices, and I would feel very depressed. And then I would just sit and watch TV and not do anything, not even read for my courses, and then I would begin to worry and think about home."

And so, little by little, Surya revealed the crisis he had been experiencing very quietly, very privately, over the last three years. No one, seeing Surya in the hall or joking with him after class, would know that he had any problems other than the usual homesickness. No one realized that criticism, even kindly criticism, felt to him like "a blow to the head." And no one imagined that asking him to write directly about the ideas of the authors he read, weighing and balancing them, was asking him to give blows to the heads of others.

Surya's story has a happy ending. He went back to Nepal with a master's degree, got married, and later came back with his wife and enrolled in the Center's doctoral program. They had a child, then another. Surya grew in stature at the Center, helping to coordinate a new summer institute for literacy professionals from all over the world. He learned to write, finally, in a style that would work for a U.S. dissertation, but only through a long struggle, by deciding that the only way he was going to survive was to analyze his own papers, noticing how they changed in response to professors' comments over the course of several years. And although he was unaware of it at the time, as his writing style changed so did his manner of speaking. One summer, when some higher-ups from the Nepali Ministry visited the Center, Surya found himself giving them some very blunt suggestions about how to run their literacy program. "I was telling them, 'This is what you should do, you have the power, you can affect the system,'" he told me. "And then I realized they were staring at me, because they never expected to be talked to that way, and I knew that the directness I had developed was really, you know, too much."

Regardless of his success in the U.S. system, Surya remains a little worried, for soon he will be going home again, and then the person he has become will not feel at ease in his old surroundings. Like many students returning from abroad, he will be caught between two cultures, at home in neither one of them. Although many who live and work in other countries are changed by the experience and feel some "reverse culture shock" upon returning home, it is learning to write within the new culture, students tell me, that produces the most profound change in a person. And this is because writing is so tied to thinking—the inner expression of a person's being—and to communicative style— its outer expression—thus touching the core of the writer's identity.

Because of the drastic nature of the change they must make, it is not surprising that some students resist academic writing or "critical thinking" when, like Surya, they begin to recognize the implications of what the U.S. university is asking them to do. Another student told me, "I was very struck when I read an article by the Chinese student who had to construct a different self-identity in order to be able to write the way Americans do. That made me think a lot. Because I *was* resistant. I had been trying to make a single identity, somehow my Japanese self and my American self merging, so I wouldn't lose the Japanese part of me. That was my fear, that I would lose my old identity, which was very important to me. Creating a new self-identity would mean that I would have to evaluate the one I originally had. And that was *such* an incredible fear! So as I read the article,[2] I guess I finally accepted that I would have to construct, in a sense, a second personality. I told myself, 'Well, I may have to.' "

Although many students describe their awareness of change and their resistance to it as growing over a number of years, others find that their most intense resistance is concentrated in a crisis period of one semester or even during the writing of a single paper. Carla, a Chilean master's student, came to me several times while writing her first paper in her new cultural context, each time with an indecipherable draft, each time telling me how stuck she felt, how impossible it was to write what she wanted to say. At the time, I had thought that it was mostly a problem with language—Carla was getting along at a pretty basic level both in speaking and writing—and with her inexperience in expressing her own opinion in a class paper. But later, reflecting on the process of writing this paper (finally finished and titled "A New Way To Write"), Carla told me how painful it had been to write in a way that felt unnatural to her and how much anxiety she had felt as she tried to force herself to adopt the style that I so cheerfully and naïvely was calling "just another technique." "I was afraid that if I forced myself to write in this new style, I would become acculturated," she told me. "But at the same time, I knew I needed to change to survive here. Personally, I was rebelling to write. The ideas didn't come."

Part of Carla's resistance was political. As she was debating with herself about the necessities and dangers of acculturation, she remembered a psychology professor she'd had in Chile who had become convinced, while doing doctoral work in the U.S., that "the American way to write" was superior to the way things were done at home. "American students do it this way," she had told her classes, "so why shouldn't you?" The students, outraged at being told that it was better to be like Americans than like themselves, had boycotted her classes, and using an empty classroom where they met on their own, chose their own course materials and designed their own examinations. "I kept thinking about what happened to that professor," said Carla, "and I thought, if I adopt this American writing style, what might become of me on my return? Will I be shunned by my own students? Or even worse, will I look down on my own people so much that I deny them their ways of communicating, their language, their way to write?"

But there is an even deeper layer to Carla's dilemma. The major difference in writing styles that she had noticed during her first semester, she told me, was that Americans tend to examine a subject very closely, as if they were looking at it under a microscope or dissecting it and describing its parts. The Latin tendency, however, is to "look at the subject from far away" and to attach great importance to the surrounding context. This difference was crucial, Carla thought, when you live under a dictatorship, for if you focus in on the subject and ignore what is going on around it, the aims of the dictatorship will be well served. Her professor's specialty was behaviorism, which had been popular in Chilean psychology departments throughout the 1970s when the Pinochet dictatorship was in full sway. "If a child is acting up in school," explained Carla, "behaviorism teaches you to look at the reinforcement the child is getting from the teacher or maybe in the home environment. But it would never question the context. Why was the teacher being aggressive with the child in the first place? Was the teacher underpaid? Was she reacting to the climate of fear? Or was the child misbehaving because his father had disappeared? Over two thousand people disappeared in four years, but if you were a behaviorist you could be blind to all that."

Thus, to Carla, this new way to write, which focused very closely and directly on the main point and walked the reader through a carefully constructed line of reasoning, ignored the diversions and distractions of the surrounding context and therefore resembled the "typically American" behaviorism that was being used in service of the U.S.-supported dictatorship.[3] Far from being a simple change in style, learning to write for the U.S. university was an act that for Carla held profound political implications. "I knew that going straight to the point would change my whole world view," Carla told me. "That made me angry. Forcing myself to change meant I was rejecting my own thoughts, the thoughts that naturally took in all the surrounding context." Some years later, after successfully adopting the style that would get her through her graduate program, Carla looked back on that paper as "the most important experience of my first semester." "As I was struggling to focus my ideas," she told me, "I drew a picture of what I wanted to say: on one side was me, writing in Chile, and on the other was me, writing here. Writing the paper helped me visualize where I was. When I could see, and really believe, that there were different ways of writing, that was the moment I could write the paper."

This breakthrough in resistance did not mean that Carla was able to immediately adopt the new style; it only signaled her willingness to try. Years later she was still working at it, slowly training herself to focus, to choose words for their precise meanings, to add the details her new audience would consider relevant. Carla tells me that her husband, who is doing a doctoral degree in economics, has never seen any compelling reason to change the way he writes. "His position is that he doesn't care," she says. "I tell him sometimes, 'If you want to be pedagogical, you have to be clear.' But he says that if things are too simple, he'll be bored. I was thinking that maybe I am more obedient to the system. I tend to adapt very well. And I don't like that," she adds, laughing a little ruefully.

Resistance to academic writing is not unique to world majority students, of course. Any student will balk, deliberately or subconsciously, when something inside, something deep and personal, is threatened or offended. Despite differences in culture and world view, human beings have in common patterns of physical and psychological growth and development, responses to power dynamics and needs for communication, any of which may call up resistance in situations that require change. Thus many world majority students resist for reasons that mainstream teachers find familiar: Yang Li, who would not do the assignment I had given him and insisted on writing on the existence of God, was, like so many eighteen-year-olds, locked in a struggle with authority, defensive to any sort of criticism, ready to argue, politely but stubbornly, that his papers did not need major alterations at all. My friend Kamala, whose writing has been blocked for years, is suffering in part from the self-doubt that afflicts so many older returning students and in part from being intellectually demeaned and censored over a long period by a partner in an unworkable relationship, an experience that can have a constricting effect on writers from any culture. World majority students who find the academic form dull or dry ("like a skeleton, there's no juicy, meaty part in it," said a Japanese student) or who are disheartened by its implicit competitiveness could join legions of U.S. graduate students who, for a time at least, resist the standard form of writing in the disciplines: the jostling for position, the veiled attacks on other authors, the name-dropping, the abandonment of common-sense vocabulary, the surrender of voice. And many women writers, including myself, could join Surya in the feeling that they cannot be expressive, cannot be convincing, unless they are personal.

But in addition to these common, shared sorts of resistance, there is a variety that is especially characteristic of world majority students: the resistance that arises from being a cultural alien in an institution that acknowledges no other but the western view. Like Surya, these students may be insulted by our ethnocentric assumptions about "good writing," which they may see as both naïve and arrogant: naïve because of our confident assumption that "good" is universal, and arrogant because even when we do acknowledge that there are other ways of thinking and communicating, we still insist that our way is the only reasonable, workable way to run the modern world. Interestingly, we even critique Japan on these grounds, while at the same time acknowledging its superiority (or at least its parity) to the U.S. in both education and business practices. A vivid example of such a critique appeared in *The New York Times* in December 1992. The U.S. and its European allies were trying to block the reelection of the Japanese director of the World Health Organization, the first Japanese ever elected head of an international agency. Dr. Hiroshi Nakajima, who is the tenth generation in his family to become a doctor, was accused of being an "incompetent administrator," a "poor leader and communicator." He cajoled and threatened other countries for their support, his American critics said; he spent too much time abroad assessing needs; "his thoughts are difficult to follow." Japanese officials countered that Nakajima's five-year term was "not long enough for his efforts to bear fruit" and threatened to reduce its funding for both the agency and its health projects worldwide if Nakajima were not reelected (Altman 1992, 1).

Neither nation understood the cultural issues involved in the dispute: in Japan, business leaders are accustomed to thinking in the long term—in decades or even life spans, long enough to build personal relationships, forge international alliances, and carefully determine needs; they find the American proclivity for the "quick fix" a little boorish and certainly inefficient in the long run. Nakajima's "autocratic style" may be better suited to a more hierarchical, collectivist system than to an egalitarian, individualistic one, and his indirect manner may have made it difficult for Americans, trained in "getting down to brass tacks," to understand where his leadership was taking the organization. The Americans' charge of incompetence insulted the Japanese government in much the same way that U.S. instructors may insult world majority students with our distinctions between "good" and "poor" academic writing.

Students who come from abroad are well aware of the "west is best" assumption prevalent in so much of U.S. diplomacy, business dealings, and foreign aid administration as well as in our teaching practices in schools and universities. Like Carla, who came of age under Pinochet's dictatorship, many world majority students are of two minds about these irritating value judgments we make and are sometimes uncomfortable about being in the U.S. at all. On the one hand, they recognize the status of a U.S. degree and are drawn to the

obvious advantages of American life: money, material goods, a greater
sense of freedom, political stability, and predictability regarding the
details of everyday life. On the other hand, they are often painfully
aware of how often "American interests abroad" have contributed to
the difficulties their countries have experienced in trying to reduce
poverty and achieve these same advantages. Students from countries
dependent on U.S. foreign aid may thus find themselves in a peculiar
position—grateful for the U.S. generosity that got them here, excited
to have realized a long-held dream, yet feeling somewhat powerless
and vulnerable to humiliation. All students of color, whether from
developing countries or not, are aware of our country's history of
racism and xenophobia and often experience such unpleasantness soon
after they arrive. Carla writes, for example, about her young daughter's
reaction to our society's implicit racism:

> She was returned from school two or three times a week. "There is
> something strange about her health," the teacher said. At first the
> doctors thought it was a cold, later they said it was an allergy. She
> was under different medications for forty-five days. One morning
> while she was taking a bath, she looked at her body and asked me,
> "Mami, yo tengo la piel brown?" Yes, I answered in Spanish. She was
> quiet for a moment, and then she started to cry. "No! No! No! Yo no
> quiero ser brown." "Why?" I asked her. "All the children at school
> are white. I don't want to be brown."
>
> My three-year-old daughter goes to a "diverse" day care with
> children from different backgrounds. But you don't have to be an
> adult to know this is a racist society. My daughter somehow knows
> that being white has a positive value in this society. Her knowledge
> comes from her body; she can feel it, her body reacts to it, she gets
> sick. It is not a coincidence that a few days later, after openly
> discussing the colors of the skin at school and at home, she became
> a healthy little girl again.

And a first-year Japanese student writes:

> I go to cut my hair. An amiable hairdresser finds my English awkward
> and asks where I am from. I answer I come from Japan. The motion
> of her hand cutting my hair rhythmically stops for seconds. A cheerful
> bus driver asks the same question. I answer. His face freezes; he
> hurriedly changes the topic politely, trying to cover his anger. Maybe
> both the hairdresser and the driver are seeing a real Japanese person
> close at hand for the first time. What is troublesome is that this kind
> of reaction is a daily matter to me. (Nakamura 1992, 11)

Such experiences, though they may seem subtle and therefore
inconsequential to those who are not subject to them, are felt by world
majority students in so many of the details of daily life that they begin
to feel uncomfortable and unwelcome. This makes some students

cautious about insidious pressures and new habits that might Americanize them, especially something as deep and powerful as a new style of writing, a new way of expressing themselves that privileges certain thoughts and disregards others. As Carla said in her first paper in my writing class, after she had broken through her resistance and forced herself to write in a way I could understand:

> *Learning to write in an American style, it is much more than learning a new technique. It is a way this culture "normalizes" you to the system, shaping on you new values and new ways of looking at the world. Therefore, the writing style is not value free; it has ethical consequences depending on if it is empowering or disempowering for you in this new culture or in your home culture.*

Clearly, resistance to academic writing is easiest to see and understand when students know exactly what they are resisting and why. This is most likely to be the case with a reflective student like Carla, who is trained in psychology and has an intense interest in her own writing process, or with a mature student like Surya, who has been an observer of cultural differences for a long time. But the situation is rarely so clear. More often, students do not understand much about their own resistance other than knowing they feel discouraged by their instructors' feedback or that they feel angry, or depressed, or anxious, or blank when they sit down to write. Few students make the connection between culture and writing and are only peripherally aware of the power issues involved, so they resist not because they resent being told they can't be themselves, but simply out of perplexity. "All you know is that everything is fixed and there are rules and you don't know what you did wrong and you are told, 'Well, you have to go straight to the point,'" says Carla. "And it made no sense to me. No sense. This way of writing had no meaning for me; it was too simple."

Perhaps my suggestion that world majority students are often unaware of how their own cultures affect them is also a bit arrogant—yes, that is a possibility. But think for a minute how difficult it is for those of us who are "western," or "westernized," to understand our own cultural assumptions and how they might affect our ways of writing and speaking. Imagine trying to pursue a higher degree in Arabic, for example, or in Japanese, and being told that your papers were organized strangely or that your most interesting ideas, your most complex thoughts, were "too simple." We too would feel insulted or discouraged or would lose confidence in our ability to say something meaningful, but we would not necessarily realize that "strange organization" is relative and that the way we were brought up to think, speak, act, and write appears "too simple" only to those who were brought up differently. Our misunderstanding would be greatest, perhaps, if we had not had much experience or success at writing in our own language and cultural context. We might then agree that we lacked practice writing, or—even more likely—that we just hadn't mastered the language well enough to express our thoughts in all their complexity. For even if we were fluent in Arabic or Japanese, we would quickly learn that it takes many years to become as creative and sophisticated as when writing in our mother tongue.

Thus we should not find it surprising if some students become convinced that they suffer from the same kinds of "writing problems" as any mainstream student and tell us they have *always* had a problem with clarity, or that their particular weakness is going off on tangents, or that they are just *terrible* at coming up with proper transitions. But if they try to correct these "writing problems" without understanding the cultural assumptions behind them, they may work at them a long time without success, wondering why they are having so much difficulty, when in their home countries, or in their other subjects, they have always been top students. And so to maintain self-respect, they may decide that it is the language itself—the vocabulary, the grammar, the turns of phrase—that is the cause of all the trouble.

This is not to downplay the real difficulties that a student may have at the level of language alone. Words or concepts can be untranslatable, equivalent verb tenses can be nonexistent or have different usage, linguistic elements can be completely absent (such as the articles "a," "an," and "the," which are absent in Chinese, Korean, Japanese, Hindi, Russian, and many other languages). In addition, because language and culture cannot easily be separated, words may contain embedded cultural information such as the place of the speaker and the audience in the social hierarchy, the mood the author wants to convey, the purpose of the piece—whether it is meant to be humorous, ironic, factual, academic—and so on.[4] Because truly mastering a language is so difficult, the idea that students who write confusing papers have "language problems" may be validated by instructors who give extensive feedback on surface errors or even suggest that the student hire an editor before submitting papers for comments on content, for mechanical details are easier to spot than the cultural differences in organization, forms of evidence, and approach to knowledge that we have been concerned with here. A typical comment of this type comes from a professor responding to a Japanese graduate student who later showed up in my writing class, deeply discouraged by her "communication problem":

> The major problem with this paper lies with the English language. The combination of overly complex style and non-idiomatic usage often leaves the reader wondering what you mean. The problem is serious enough that your message and analysis, which is often quite good, is generally lost in language. In short, you have to work on expressing yourself in written English. This is a problem which you must solve in order to proceed with your graduate studies. Until you address the writing problems, people will often not see the quality or the value of your approach. I know written English is difficult, but it is a valuable skill in today's world. I look forward to your next paper.

This focus on linguistic correctness may then actually invite frustration and resentment; students may complain that they are spending too much of their time abroad "learning English" and not enough on course content or on the research that they came to do. They may complain bitterly that they are being unfavorably compared with native speakers just because of language differences. "I'm being really put down here," says a Nepali student, "and I'm being considered nothing just because of the fact that I cannot express myself in English." "I got a lot of red marks on my paper," adds an Indonesian student, "and that made me lose my self-confidence. The professor said, 'You are struggling with the language.' That was true, I *know* I have a problem with English, but when he said that, I felt really miserable." "If you would create less havoc about the language and give more importance to the ideas," the Nepali student adds, "it would really benefit us more." But as we have seen, teaching the ideas separately from the way they are thought about and communicated is a hopeless endeavor, for language and culture cannot be separated.

Resistance to U.S. academic style is not confined to newcomers. As U.S. society becomes more tolerant of the expression of cultural differences and exerts somewhat less pressure on immigrants to conform to the mainstream, and as the racism, violence, and other deficiencies of the American way of life become more apparent, more and more families of world majority students are creating cultural havens inside their homes, speaking their maternal language, keeping to their traditions, maintaining familiar ways of understanding and responding to the world. Children of these families sometimes become "Americanized" anyway, influenced by school, friends, television, and spending money. But a surprising number are resisting assimilation, so we may encounter students who were born in the U.S. or who came here when they were tiny, yet who speak and write in English with more difficulty than some newcomers. Or such students may speak English fluently and act like any mainstream teenager, but have the same difficulties with writing, for the same reasons, as students who have grown up abroad.

Christine is one such student; she came into Writing Workshop one evening with a three-paragraph statement of her educational goals on an application for a science scholarship. "It's being offered by a drug company," she told me, wrinkling up her nose in mild distaste. "But it's money," she shrugged. Her spoken English is fluent; she has no accent to speak of. She was born in the U.S. to parents who had immigrated from the People's Republic of China and has come to the university as an honor student from a U.S. high school.

I look at her first paragraph; about all I can decipher is that she plans to go to medical school four years from now. When I ask her to just tell me what she wants to say, she thinks deeply, smiles, and says again the words she has written. She thinks in Cantonese, she tells me, especially when she writes. Her grammar is surprisingly poor for a high achiever who has lived in the U.S. all her life. In the few simple sentences she is trying to put together, she uses the present tense when she needs the present perfect ("I work in emergency room last two years"), confuses adjectives with adverbs, and draws a blank when I ask her for words to describe more precisely her volunteer hospital experience. Cantonese is her first language, she tells me in answer to my question; she began learning English when she was six. She is studying German now so that she will be able to read the medical literature when she becomes a doctor. German is her fourth language, she says, glancing at me to see if I will catch her meaning.

"What is your third language?" I ask.

"There's some Spanish in my life," she replies, smiling mysteriously.

I ask her to explain. "I was put in a bilingual class that met during recess time in second grade. All the other kids were Spanish. I don't know why they put me in there. I guess I look a little Spanish," she shrugs again, smiling. "My parents were told the class would help me. They were immigrants, and many things were confusing to them, but they did what the school told them to do."

Although her Spanish instruction ended after fourth grade, Christine continued in ESL classes throughout elementary and high school, mainly to improve her grammar. But her grammar did not improve, nor did she begin thinking in English when she wrote, something that comes naturally to many students as they become immersed in the language. I realize, near the end of the half hour I have with her, that Christine has no trouble thinking in English when she talks about everyday matters; it is her writing that needs translation. I soon realize why: the ideas and values that she most cherishes are expressed in

Cantonese at home. Her father is an herbalist, she tells me, and she wants to continue the family tradition by combining eastern and western approaches to medicine. Her grandmother's Cantonese dialect, a form not widely spoken, dominates the home. Even television, that great acculturizer, has been replaced in her family by videos from Taiwan. So when she tries to articulate something as serious as her educational goals, she thinks about them the way she thinks about all serious matters at home: in Cantonese.

I look again at the three paragraphs. "Christine," I say gently, "don't you think you should get to work on your English? Especially if you want to become a doctor, you'll certainly want to communicate in writing . . . " But Christine has all sorts of reasons why she cannot work on her English right now. She has to take her Cantonese class so that she'll learn the standard dialect and be able to read the Chinese medical literature. And then there's her German class, so really there is no time to improve her English grammar. And as for making new friends to talk with about the ideas she is learning at the university, most of her friends speak Cantonese, and she doesn't really have much interest in meeting anyone else.

Christine is resisting not only academic writing, but the dominant language and culture, even as she sets high goals for herself as a professional in that culture. And so I straighten out her three paragraphs as best I can without suggesting more grammar classes, without mentioning style—at least not in this brief meeting, for I will make no headway unless Christine finds a reason to be open to the idea of change.

Every student's resistance is different. Resistance can make naturally vague writing even more so. It can cause English vocabulary to slip away when a student needs it most. It can cause depression and anxiety, which in turn can create writer's block. Resistance does not always silence, though; it can cause a student to throw as many words as possible at the page without knowing or caring if they make sense. "I'd be sitting in front of the computer with a cup of coffee," says a Japanese graduate student, "getting all psyched and nervous, thinking, 'Oh my gosh, what am I going to do?' just trying to be productive and filling up pages." Resistance can even cause a student to be magnificently articulate and produce an angry tirade in place of the expected cool, objective prose. A Tanzanian doctoral student writes:

> *Western policy-makers have now come up with yet another solution to all the world's problems: No children! Like its many predecessors, this policy is meant for all Third World countries regardless of the facts pertaining to each country. Is it based on the fears of the western*

*leaders that the Third World will take control of the world by using
sheer numbers? Probably!*

Resistance can cause a peculiar lack of attention to simple grammar
errors, the rules for which the student learned years ago. It can cause
a student to disagree, sometimes politely, sometimes hotly, with every
change the instructor suggests, thus making substantial revision of the
draft impossible. And resistance is mutable; it may first appear as
totally disconnected prose, then change to writer's block, perhaps
accompanied by an angry, insulted stance, then turn to panic and self-
doubt, then to overwriting—an abundance of words and quotes and
half-formed ideas for far too many pages. Or it may take an entirely
different sequence. Like a cornered animal, resistance will dash for
whatever path is open to it. Because whether it is angry, or polite, or
depressed, or panicked, or blithe and uncaring, or devious, or contin-
ually confused, resistance to academic writing has one primary function
for a writer with different cultural assumptions—to avoid the inevitable
changes in personality, outlook, and world view that go hand in hand
with the new writing style.

Not all world majority students are resistant, of course. Some, like
Shu Ming, a freshman who came from the People's Republic of China
when she was seven, remembering only that "the TV commercials
there weren't fun, like here," are only too willing to adopt a style that
makes them sound "more American." I had been carefully trying to
preserve her poetic voice, her delicate rhetorical questions, keeping
my comments to a minimum in conference, suggesting changes sometimes but then retreating from them, not wanting to stifle her sweet,
almost birdsong expression. Though Shu Ming never asked me for
more direction, she was more open to change than I had imagined (or
hoped) she would be. One day just before her portfolio was due, she
went for some last-minute help from a peer tutor[5] and learned, in a
matter of half an hour, what I had been trying so hard not to impose
upon her. In a piece reflecting on her writing process she recounts
what happened:

How I Tried To Attack The Weakness Of My Paper

*Oh how frustrating the assignment has become! After I heard the
peer tutor's comments, I felt like crying and throwing the paper into
the sky. Sitting down again with the fourth draft of my "Freedom of
Speech and Flag Desecration" paper, I started to think about the
advice of my tutor. The problems I had with my paper all started
from asking too many rhetorical questions. Although it is all right to
use the style, asking too many questions will make the reader wonder
about my main focus. Instead, I need to make some questions into
statements and say what I want to say.*

> *Other problems I had with the paper were based on coherence. In order to attack my weakness, I should state my thesis, tell the reader my thoughts, and expand my paper from there. During the course of writing each supportive paragraph, I need to think about the topic sentence and clearly list the reasons to back it up, and think about how others will argue against my point, so the readers won't be able to poke any hole in my writing. Upon finishing the paragraph, I should make sure each supportive statement is focused on the topic sentence. By writing concisely, the paper will seem to be strongly linked, which in turn will give a strong argumentative paper.*
>
> *Writing any type of paper is a step-by-step organizing. Although it takes a lot of thought it is worth the effort. I can't believe how much the peer tutor has helped me—looking at my first draft I just can't believe how each draft has progressed.*

While Shu Ming mentions that "it is all right to use [her former] style," her language implies that she will not use it for long: "too many rhetorical questions," "attack my weaknesses," "how each draft has progressed." Indeed, Shu Ming came back to visit me at the end of the next semester to show me several *A* papers she had written for an advanced literature class. The difference in her work was striking: she had developed a confident tone, eliminated many of her surface errors, and tied her complex argument tightly together the way she tells herself to do in the above passage.

Though Shu Ming is engaged in rejecting her former ways of expressing herself, other students manage to view the change they are experiencing as additive. Maria, for example, a graduate student from Brazil, says she is happy to have a variety of styles in her repertoire. Though change has been slow for her, she has not worried much about it, not even noticed it particularly, until her parents pointed out that her letters were sounding different, even in Portuguese, and her friends began to laugh at the way her voice sounded on the phone. "My friends say, 'Maria, it's something weird the way you're talking now.' I think it's my storytelling style; I'm much more specific than the way I used to be. Even my tone of voice is not going up and down as much; it's more linear."

Why is resistance almost a non-issue for some students while it stops others in their tracks? My guess is that the degree of difficulty a student has in adopting U.S. style might hinge on a number of factors: the degree of similarity or dissimilarity of thought and expression between the two cultures (Russian students having less difficulty understanding what the differences are than Koreans or Japanese); the degree of the family's "westernization" in their home or home country (many undergraduates at this institution come from elite families who have internalized a western outlook and may speak only English to each other); the degree of westernization in the students' previous education, some schools being more western-oriented than others; the degree of the students' adaptability to other cultures (or, as Carla might say, "their obedience to the system"); their experience with western racism or colonialism; and numerous personal factors: their individual goals for education, their response to criticism, their sociability, and their experiences with individual faculty members, who may poison their stay here with tactless remarks and assumptions, or be as supportive, patient, and generous with their time as Surya's adviser— who, as Surya said at his goodbye party, "was like a second father to me."

Many students manage to overcome their resistance, for they are determined to succeed in this context; they face, as Surya says, "the terrible value their families place on success." Others hire editors or work intensely with devoted thesis advisers in order to make just enough changes in the writing to satisfy their dissertation committees. Some gravitate to mathematics, computer science, engineering, and other scientific fields that do not depend so much on writing. And many, I suspect, return home without being changed significantly by their writing, because they have not had to do enough of it to bring the questions, the contradictions, the clash in values to the surface.

But some groups of world majority students have no home country to return to or remember and therefore have different perceptions of what American education and culture can do for them. These groups, which educational anthropologist John Ogbu calls "involuntary minorities," have been made a part of U.S. society through slavery, conquest, or colonization and have been assigned menial status within it. And according to this Nigerian observer of the U.S. scene, this position can call forth the most powerful resistance of all . . .

6 Stigma and Resistance

Joella has been sent to Writing Workshop by an instructor in the minority support program; the terse note I find in her file says, "Not motivated to write." The other sins listed are standard: *-ed* endings, plurals, comma splices. She's dressed to kill: stylish hat, expensive-looking outfit. She has a big voice, a big smile, and provocative ways, convincing ways. She half-closes her eyes and slouches first to one side and then, with a dramatic shift, to the other. She laughs when I show her the Writing Workshop slip. "Not motivated. *She* said that? Well it's true, I'm not. But I try though. Really I do."

I ask her about her background; she tells me she's been failing. Her hometown? "Detroit, born and raised." Her aspirations? To work, not sure at what. She has a work-study job now, at the medical center, and hates it. "It's so boring. I file, and then there's nothing to do. So I write my papers on the job." She looks up at me, incredulous that these meager duties should count as "work." I ask her what she feels her writing problems are. "Well, I write like I talk, that's one thing." No apologies, she just does. "And grammar." She shows me her draft, a story for a creative writing class. It's pretty clean—but "you should have seen it before." I assume she got help from the writing teachers over at minority support.

Her story is sassy, sexy, and totally irreverent; it's about a woman with a series of boyfriends, the best of whom had a huge and mysterious source of cash to pay for her favors, all the while engaged to someone else. I find a few places that need smoothing—some logical inconsistencies and, in the latter part of the paper, a fair amount of grammatical confusion. She knows the rules, though, better than most of my mainstream students do. "Comma splice," she says when I pause at one. She knows what parallelism is and uses semicolons correctly, though the difference between "pass," "past," and "passed" is still very confusing to her. These difficulties seem trivial to me; though much is made of them in the university, it doesn't seem as if they should present an insurmountable barrier to her success. As I compare Joella's text in my mind with a dissertation proposal brought to me by an international graduate student the previous hour, the number of surface errors and the difficulty applying well-remembered rules are about the same. And beneath the language interference and sentence-level problems, Joella's text is strong.

As we read on through her story and meet more of its outrageous characters, the street slang comes out strong and clear. "The dialect sounds great here," I tell her, "but I think it's better to stick to standard grammar when the narrator is telling us something. Try to hold on to the tone, don't lose your great metaphors ("He was the color of caramels, the kind you buy in bulk") but get in all of those -*ed* endings." I'm not sure if this is right, stylistically, but it was the way she started the paper, and it seems logical to hold to the pattern.

I love this voice, so unrepentantly bad. "He would give me five hundred a week, just for spending money, laid out two thousand for my tuition. He's got money up the butt." As we laugh, she becomes animated, and I realize that all the "unmotivated" tone has gone out of her voice. For a few moments she is engaged, ready to be taken seriously as a writer. But after a few strong pages, the draft peters out, and with it, her careful, focused attention. Intelligent, talented, bored with her menial status, and privy to all the resources of an outstanding university, Joella has everything she needs to make it. Yet she is failing, and no amount of special counseling or writing help will suddenly and miraculously turn that around. "I know I need to improve my writing," she tells me at the end of the half hour. "I want a more interesting job than the one I've got now. I'm trying, really I am."

Joella's stance and performance are not uncommon among those whom anthropologist John Ogbu calls "involuntary minorities"— groups that have been incorporated into a society against their will and assigned a subordinate and despised position within it.[1] Korean students, an involuntary minority in Japan, are doing poorly there, about as poorly as African Americans, Native Americans, and Puerto Ricans are doing in the U.S. But when they come to this country, Korean students flourish as a "model minority," surpassing U.S. mainstream students in college attendance rates and achievement-test scores.[2]

The reason for this surprising difference in performance, Ogbu suggests, is that the Koreans who come to make their home here do so voluntarily, in search of a better life. Though they suffer from U.S. racism and discrimination as do all people of color, and though they must learn to get along in a new language, they tend to view these difficulties as "obstacles to overcome" rather than permanent barriers to their success. When they think about their homeland, they know they would have fewer opportunities there, so no matter how difficult their new life in the U.S. might be, it seems preferable to the one they left behind. But the Koreans who settled in Japan did not do so of their own free will. In the early 1900s, Korean laborers had become so impoverished by Japan's colonial policies that they were forced to flee to the very country that had exploited them. Forced immigration began in earnest at the beginning of World War II, when Koreans were brought to Japan as indentured laborers and military conscripts, denied equal opportunities for education, and held in open contempt by Japanese society. Today, Koreans continue to suffer severe discrimination in schooling, housing, and employment.[3] Although Korean parents have high expectations for their children's future, fewer than 10 percent of Korean college graduates find work in Japanese-owned companies,[4] and only those who have become Japanese citizens can be hired by public institutions, including schools and colleges, public corporations, and national and local governments.[5] Koreans sometimes try to "pass" as Japanese by using Japanese names at school, but if their identity is discovered, they are made objects of ridicule by Japanese children, who are taught to look down on Koreans and their culture. Nor do Japanese teachers hold high expectations for Korean children, possibly because they know they must "be realistic" about their future employability. As a despised minority in a country they distrust, Koreans in Japan do not have the heart to push themselves to the limit of their abilities. Like Joella, they try, but something inside is saying no.

Even more interesting is the case of the Burakumin, a Japanese minority group within Japan, whose educational performance and social stigmatization have been studied by Nobuo Shimahara (1991) of Rutgers University. Though the Burakumin are not immigrants to Japan, they can be seen as an involuntary minority in the sense that they were assigned "permanently unchangeable" status as a pariah group in feudal Japan in the early 1600s, assigned to pick up garbage, handle dead animals, and perform other unskilled and lowly tasks. Though the Burakumin were emancipated in 1892 at the beginning of the Meiji Restoration and assigned status as "new commoners," their place in society remained unchanged until very recently. Before serious efforts were made by the government to integrate this group into Japanese mainstream society (largely as a result of the Burakumin's militant struggle for equality), they remained poor and were notoriously low achievers whose "deep-seated problem," according to their teachers, was cognitive deficiency in reading, writing, and mathematics. Burakumin made up an abnormally high percentage of students in special education classes in elementary and middle schools.[6] In fact, there seemed to be a significant gap in IQ scores between the Burakumin and mainstream Japanese children. Before their dramatic improvement in social mobility and educational attainment in the 1970s, an enormous percentage of Burakumin lived on welfare: 70 percent in 1964, compared with less than 6 percent of the mainstream Japanese. Their ghetto housing was dilapidated and often physically separated from that of the dominant group. Common occupations: junk dealer, peddler, factory worker, unemployed.

It is important to note that the Burakumin have absolutely no differences about them that would distinguish them from mainstream Japanese; their physical appearance, language, ethnicity, and culture are identical with those of the majority. Burakumin could only be identified by their place of residence, which, until the 1970s, had to be recorded in a family registry that was open to public inspection. Job applications also required that individuals state their specific place of birth, a practice that was used to foster discrimination against Burakumin in the workplace.

Until such practices were outlawed and a vigorous program of "assimilation education" was instituted by the government, few Burakumin made it to the high school level. But with new programs for teacher training, financial aid, special counseling, equal opportunities for employment for Burakumin youth, and instruction of mainstream children about discrimination and prejudice, educational attainment of the Burakumin "has risen phenomenally."[7] And when Burakumin come to the U.S. as voluntary immigrants, Ogbu says, they have been as successful as other Japanese without any specialized help at all.

The Koreans and Burakumin in Japan, then, suffer similar treatment and develop similar responses to their fate as do African Americans, Native Americans, and some Hispanic groups in the U.S. These comparative studies suggest that it is not racism per se that is the cause of poor educational performance, for even "model minorities" suffer from America's color consciousness. Nor is it poverty, or language, or cultural differences that are the biggest barriers to success. The key issues are the way the group came to be a part of the "host" culture, the status they were assigned, and their response, as a group, to this predicament.[8]

Because involuntary minorities do not enter a society with hopes for improving their lives, they do not, when the chips are down, compare their situation favorably with the one they left behind. They can only contrast their status with that of the dominant group and conclude that they are worse off largely because of their involuntary membership in a disparaged group. They do not see much opportunity for upward mobility; while other immigrant groups see their situations as temporary, involuntary minorities see the discrimination against them as institutionalized and permanent. Thus, Ogbu says, despite their high aspirations and interest in education, children of involuntary minorities may not develop the most effective strategies for achievement in school, for they feel that no matter how hard they work, they will never gain the same opportunities for professional advancement, the same respect as human beings, as any of the other immigrant groups that came of their own free will (Ogbu 1991b).

To add to their difficulties, Ogbu says, schools unconsciously prepare such students to accept low social and economic status by neglecting to challenge them or reward them appropriately for their efforts. For example, in a study of African Americans in Stockton, California, Ogbu found that elementary children of the majority were given grades that reflected their level of achievement, but African American and Mexican American children were consistently given Cs and Ds (locally known as "the average grade"), regardless of their performance—though written comments by teachers about individual children's performance indicated that there was a wider variation among students than their grades indicated. Since greater individual effort did not seem to be associated with better grades, parents did not insist that their children work hard, and the children set low goals for their own performance, tending to blame the system when they achieved less than their mainstream classmates (Ogbu 1991c).

This response of involuntary minorities to their ascribed status is similar, it seems to me, to the attitude of women as a group towards achievement—not in school necessarily, where nowadays we are expected to match or even outdo males, but afterwards, in the career world. It is here that women still tend to give up too easily, telling each other that the barriers we face are just too tough: the "old boy network," the lack of affordable child care, the difficulties in pursuing top jobs in other areas of the country because of duties to husbands or aging parents, and so on. Though there is no denying that these barriers are real, under other circumstances we might see them as "obstacles to overcome" rather than reasons for our comparatively low collective achievement. But because we have internalized the historical notion of how much achievement is appropriate for women, we may set our gauge at a lower level than is warranted, resigning ourselves to the non-tenure-track position, the lower profile within the department, the part-time job, the role of "helpmate."

Women respond like involuntary minorities when we think of ourselves in our role as "woman" (regardless of whether we carry additional burdens of race or class) because we, too, are part of a society that considers us inferior yet expects our loyalty and enthusiastic participation. Like African Americans, our status is ascribed to us at birth and we suffer social and economic discrimination as a result of it. Because we do not have a "homeland situation of former selves" (Ogbu 1991a, 16), we can compare ourselves only to the privileged majority (in this case, men) and conclude that we are worse off, as a group, simply because of our gender. We, too, are sent ambivalent messages as adolescents: excelling in school will get you to the top later in life, but at the same time you might as well set your sights lower, because care for others will always have to take precedence over your own achievements. We, too, adopt coping mechanisms that tend to blame the system instead of just putting our heads down and trudging against the wind the way "voluntary minorities" do in order to achieve at the highest levels. I am not trying to suggest a strict parallel here between women and involuntary minorities, for women as a group have never suffered birth-ascribed "pariah status"—the collective and enduring contempt and disgust of the majority group and resulting discrimination in every major aspect of life. I draw the comparison only to suggest a point of empathy.

Just as men who are sympathetic to women's issues often have real difficulty understanding why some of their attitudes and remarks are seen as sexist, so mainstream students and instructors do not always find it easy to understand how we unconsciously participate in the disparagement of involuntary minorities, or to realize just how powerful are the effects of the most subtle abuse.[9] Ogbu gives an everyday example from his research in Stockton: white residents commonly made a distinction between certain kinds of people called "nontax-payers," who lived in neighborhoods with low assessed property values where many people were on welfare, and other kinds of people called "taxpayers," who lived in affluent neighborhoods with few or no welfare recipients. Since blacks generally lived in low income neighborhoods, says Ogbu, they were automatically classified as "nontax-payers," regardless of whether or not they actually paid the usual taxes on sales, income, or property. Elaborate media coverage was given to the responsible concerns of "taxpayers," while those classified as "nontaxpayers" were commonly portrayed as dependent and incompetent, requiring the help and endless patience of "taxpayers" to rehabilitate them into useful citizens (Ogbu 1991c).

Insulting generalizations like these, born of neighborhood gossip and perpetuated by the media, eventually make their way into university classrooms where, dressed up in social science terminology, they give unconscious authority to the lingering traces of racism in even the most liberal of students and instructors. The fear of and contempt for black men, for example, a pervasive motif in white society since the days of slavery, creates in the classroom the stereotypical construct of "the black father," habitually absent, unemployed, involved in crime or drugs, perhaps in jail—in any case, a "poor role model" for young black men. Though statistics verify that black men have high unemployment rates and are disproportionately represented in the criminal justice system, the image of male absence or general incompetence in the ordinary black family is so pervasive that it has become an unquestioned "fact" to many students and instructors. So easily do we accept such "facts" that we may be a little taken aback by a determined student who takes it upon himself to refute them:

> *"Every man is innocent until proven guilty." This is one of the basic rights that all people supposedly have living in the United States. But this right is not given to all people. Because of the many stereotypes that exist in the United States, many people are presumed to be guilty of certain things simply on the basis of their skin color. . . . One of the most common stereotypes of the black father is that he is irresponsible and that he doesn't support or take care of his family. I disagree with this depiction of the black father. My father, Malcolm Laney, does assume his responsibilities and supports his family. When my mother lost her job, for instance, my father worked longer hours to make up for the lost income. . . . But the media rarely show this kind of situation; they show a black father running out on his family or abandoning them, putting them on welfare. . . .*
>
> *Society has another stereotype of the black father, which is that he is focused on himself and his own pleasure and doesn't care about the future generations. My father cares a great deal about the future generations of our family. After a long day's work he sits down and helps his seven-year-old granddaughter with her math homework or spelling. . . . With these shared moments, my father is giving his granddaughter a precious gift: a positive image of black men that she will never forget.*
>
> *. . . The media, racism, and the ignorance of people have created these stereotypes of the black father. I know of many other black fathers who are just like my father, and <u>they</u> are the ones who are typical of the vast majority of black fathers in the United States. If a person asked me to show him what most black fathers are like, I would show him my father—a hard-working, loving, caring man who takes care of his responsibilities, a man who is completely unlike the black father that the media have tried and convicted. (Laney 1993, 27)*

But students may not feel comfortable enough in the classroom to write such a piece, or to put in the work it takes to make it as clear and polished and as cognizant of the subtleties of audience as it needs to be, especially when that audience is largely white. When derogatory stereotypes—however innocently presented—pervade the classroom, many black students become angry and frustrated, unable to argue against the greater knowledge of their professors or the assumptions of the wider society. Another student, trying to write a paper for her composition class about a slide presentation in an anthropology lecture that depicted early humans with white skin and European features, despite their origin in East Africa, was so upset that she was unable to redraft her paper, much less sit down and talk with the anthropology professor as her writing instructor had suggested. The imbalance of power—between student and professor, between black and white, between emotion and science—was too great; the result was a hastily prepared paper, uninformed and full of surface errors, exactly the kind of essay that reinforced the stereotype the student was trying so hard to fight.

This kind of subtle assault on the sensibilities of involuntary minority students may also be perpetuated by classmates, most of whom would deny any feelings of prejudice. For example, in my freshman writing class I might have a white student or a student from a "voluntary" minority background arguing against affirmative action on the grounds that students who are poorly prepared "just can't cut it at a good school"—in a paper so sloppily written, so full of grammatical errors and lack of evidence that I need to insist on a series of extra conferences to keep the student from failing. Or I will have a white student, no better prepared, who will shake his head in dismay when reading the paper of his African American classmate, assuming that the paper's faults are a result of poor, inner-city schooling and therefore somehow worse than his own.

Mainstream students may be so used to making these kinds of assumptions and remarks that they have no idea they are offensive. A white student reads from his essay a passage he considers humorous: *"Euthanasia is the ultimate in lack of concern for the patient. You might as well drop him off in downtown Detroit and let nature take its course."* When a black student, with my encouragement, tells him that the comparison offends her, he offers to change "Detroit" to "New York City" in order not to appear prejudiced against her home town. A black student, in my office for a letter of recommendation to a sorority in the black Greek system, gives me an example of what she considers her outspoken nature—not sure if that is good or bad. In her environmental science class a white student had remarked that "Detroit is empty, because everyone has moved out." The mostly white class had laughed, and another white student had added that things are changing now because "people" are beginning to move back from the suburbs again. "I had to say—because I live there—that Detroit has never been empty," Sondra tells me, her eyes flashing. "But I only said that because the class laughed," she quickly adds. "I don't think the students' remarks were purposely racist, just unthinking. It was strange though— the TA said, 'Let's not get racial now,' and stopped the discussion."

Though Sondra feels that such remarks are not intentional or mean enough to be called racist, I would disagree. White liberals since my childhood in the 1950s have decried racist epithets and overt discrimination while finding perfectly acceptable a set of internal assumptions and judgments about blacks, Hispanics, and Native Americans— Ogbu's "involuntary minorities." This "acceptable" level of racism is so ingrained in the thinking of ordinary, kind, educated people that those of us who are not the objects of it may not find it remarkable or recognize it as derogatory.[10] The constant, daily disparagement: the silence, the knowing look, the snicker, the averting of the eyes ("I started smiling at white students on campus," says Sondra, "and counting how many smiled back") can wear down the spirit of even top involuntary minority students, who are dropping out of college in appalling numbers. One study at a large, prestigious university found that black students with top SAT scores (combined scores of 1,400) are much more likely than whites with the same test scores to flunk out, 18 to 33 percent of blacks compared with 2 to 11 percent of whites (C. Steele 1992, 70). "Something depresses black achievement *at every level of preparation, even the highest,*" says Claude Steele, professor of social psychology at Stanford. "The culprit I see is stigma, the endemic devaluation many blacks face in our society and schools" (68).[11]

"Our unconscious belief in our inferiority has grown worse over the years," said author Bebe Moore Campbell (1993) in an address to students on Martin Luther King Day. "Its symptom is constant anger." The low esteem in which black Americans are held has been turned inward, creating feelings of unworthiness, self-pity, depression, "shame and rage within our families," "scapegoating of our mates"—the "race pain" that is "the emotional legacy of our slave heritage." "We are America's abused children," she told the hushed audience. "We seek healing, not because we are sick, but because we have been wounded."[12]

Though many involuntary minority students have suffered the emotional abuse of racism since they were very young, others are struck down at adolescence, just when they are beginning to believe that people might one day live together in peace and mutual respect despite their differences, that "multiculturalism" is possible. Kendra, a privileged black student from a wealthy suburb, is trying to write, as she says, "a dialectic argument to discover the motivations of my best friend's parents." When she was twelve, she writes, she and a white neighbor "swore eternal friendship that would transcend the boundaries of race and religion and create a world of true harmony." But the neighborhood was changing: more people of color were moving in and whites were fleeing to more distant suburbs. And then one day the friend, too, was moving away. The friend's parents, who had always encouraged the children's idealism, were vague about the reasons they were leaving. And although the friend assured Kendra that she would call every day, soon her calls stopped, and Kendra's attempts at communication were intercepted by the friend's mother. Five years later, Kendra is still intensely angry, trying to make sense of the family's behavior. Was it the racism in society that had finally corrupted them, she wonders, or did they always wear masks, their pious words about harmony concealing "an Archie Bunker mentality"? As we work through the paper, I can see that despite Kendra's capabilities and training, it is extremely difficult for her to construct a formal argument on such a painful topic. It would be so much easier for her to discuss something simple, like abortion, or AIDS, or what to do with drunk drivers. But she is intent on staying with the subject; she needs answers in order to put her mind at rest. As I listen, Kendra half reads, half tells me the story, the confusion in her text mirroring her agitated thoughts. There is little I can do in my half hour with her but ask questions, and speculate with her, and listen. I don't expect that she will be able to work through enough of her feelings by next Tuesday, when her draft is due, to shape this angry confusion into a sober dialectical argument. But I wonder what her paper will look like to her instructor, who believes he has given the class a straightforward assignment: to apply a particular form of argumentation to a topic of the student's choice.

Like other sensitive, intelligent, disillusioned students, Kendra may carry such unresolved feelings with her all her life, the painful questions they evoke intensifying as she reaches higher and higher levels of achievement. Indeed, the most successful students are sometimes the most vulnerable: the Native American transfer student from a community college who is totally convinced that his occasional trouble elaborating his ideas in writing is evidence that he doesn't belong at a top university; the black Ph.D. student whose tendency to procrastinate is magnified in her own eyes until it seems to justify the pain she feels in her daily encounters with the "acceptable" level of racism. These students are experiencing what Steele calls a "double vulnerability around failure—the fear they lack ability, and the dread that they will be devalued" (1992, 75). So even though their writing problems may be no worse than those of their classmates, involuntary minority students may be a good deal more reluctant to expose their weaknesses, afraid to give their instructors yet another confirmation of what has been branded on their foreheads at birth: stupid, incapable, "not fit to be assimilated."[13]

A student sits in the darkened corner beside my desk, reading to me in a small, hoarse voice. Her assignment for a sociology class is to compare social theory and biological theory to explain black school failure. Each time I stop her, asking for more information, she retreats into herself a little more, shrinking into her oversized coat, which she has declined to take off, even in the overheated office. Her draft is confused, incomplete; Jensen's genetic inferiority argument is not well summarized, much less compared in any reasonable depth to social theory. I tell her she needs to read more, that she needs to find a good strong critique of Jensen out there in the literature in order to understand and better articulate the argument. I offer to show her how to get onto the library computer system to find a rebuttal of Jensen's theory. But she is too frightened to begin. Her hands are trembling as she packs up her books and papers, embarrassment sweeping like waves over the rocks of fear and dread. What if she can't understand it? What if it's true?

There are different stances, of course, different coping mechanisms. "I'm writing an argument on modern-day lynchings," another freshman announces as she settles herself into my office chair.

"And what is your position?" I ask.

She looks me straight in the eye. "That they do exist. Yes." She nods emphatically and gives the desk a measured tap, like a conductor.

"And are you going to bring in Clarence Thomas?" I ask, smiling a little. "No, no! I wouldn't give that man the time of day. He is *very* disrespectful of women." She relaxes a little, gives me a broad smile. It is easier when we can imagine a shared enemy.

But neither stance—neither fear and avoidance nor brazen risk-taking—is likely to put the student into the frame of mind for the sustained pattern of preparation these papers require: research, read, plan, draft, rethink, redraft, and so on. It is easier, sometimes, with the tangle of emotions inside, to take Joella's tack, to put in a minimum of effort and then allow yourself to drift toward failure. Often, these

talented but underachieving students are surprised when college instructors insist they work harder on their writing. "In high school, if
I handed in all my papers, I got *As*," Joella says, a remark echoed by
students from both inner-city and suburban schools. Wayne, a top
athlete who had been sheltered and cultivated by a private high school
in an affluent community, attributes his invented spelling and serious
reading difficulties to "silly mistakes" and becomes more confused
and angry each time he fails introductory composition, refusing to
spend more time on his drafts or to get himself tested for learning
disabilities. Though obviously intelligent, Wayne's potential for intellectual achievement has been seriously compromised by his high school
teachers, who not only let him slide by grade after grade in reading
and writing, but *never let him know* that his performance was not on
the same level as that of his classmates.

And so Wayne sits in my office (and later, after he failed my class,
in the office of his next writing instructor) astounded to hear that he
is not prepared for college-level courses, refusing to believe that he
needs to do anything more than make minor changes in the wording
of his skimpy essays, angry at all six instructors who have been called
on, one after the other, to evaluate his work and who have each
determined that he needs to learn to elaborate, to create some complexity, to read and research independently of his tutors (specially
provided by the athletic department) before he will have the skills he
needs to compete at the university he chose, in his words, "for its
combination of academics and athletics." And I am left angry, too, not
with Wayne, who despite all his blaming and complaining is still quite
a likable young person, but with his former school, which has shown
him such profound disrespect.

Because of their stigmatization, then, involuntary minority students
are more likely than students from other ethnic groups to have a
frightening, angry experience in the university, an experience that may
cause them to "disidentify" with achievement, changing their outlook
and values so that their self-esteem comes from sources other than
academics (Steele 1992, 74). The terms under which they were incorporated into mainstream society—the despised position they were
assigned, the demeaning of their every human characteristic—are so
powerfully negative that even the most talented students may lower
their internal hopes and expectations. They may then have trouble
trusting their own ideas, or rereading a difficult text when they don't
understand it the first time, or applying their knowledge of grammar
and punctuation to sentence-level problems, or feeling even marginally
at home in an institution that welcomes them not because it believes

in them, but because it needs to foster an image of diversity and equal opportunity.

The resistance of involuntary minority students is complicated, because it is not only academic writing they are uneasy about but mainstream culture itself. On university campuses this resistance is sometimes expressed as militancy—loud, defiant in-group behavior, with severe penalties for those who attempt to defect to mainstream society by dating white students, speaking Standard English, or spending too much time in the library or the lab. For students who come from impoverished neighborhoods, resistance can be compounded by the guilt that may accompany crossing class lines (incurring the resentment or ridicule of friends and family) or from "survival conflict" (Whitten 1992), a subconscious reaction to surpassing the accomplishments of brothers and sisters who are left to struggle with the poverty, drugs, and violence in their neighborhoods and the early death of their hopes and dreams. When these students travel between the two communities, the physically safe and comfortable (but emotionally dangerous) one of the college dormitory and the more violent and uncomfortable (but emotionally welcoming) one of a poverty-stricken neighborhood, they may feel a great deal of tension and internal conflict, which in turn increases the tendency toward self-sabotage. Thanksgiving is a particularly difficult time for many first-semester students who come from the inner city; on the one hand, they are relieved to be going home, but on the other, they must face the feelings of betrayal of friends left behind.

These complex forms of resistance and the reasons behind them are really quite different from the resistance of other world majority students, especially those who have come from abroad to go to school on U.S. campuses. Though international students may have similar reactions to U.S. racism or to the effects of colonialism, their resistance is, for the most part, neither as violent nor as detrimental to their own progress. Since undergraduates who have come to the U.S. for the purpose of studying in a university are generally from middle- or upper-class backgrounds, or are elite or specially chosen students if they come from socialist countries, psychological stress over class issues is minimal. And when international students face survival conflict, as they sometimes do, the traumatic situations they have escaped by coming to the U.S. for an education—famine, drought, military crackdowns, ethnic or religious violence, civil war—are not fraught with confusion and ambivalence but are clear to everyone. "I don't think about home much," an Angolan student told me when I asked about her family. "With the war, there is no food, no food at all. I don't know how they survive. But if I think about it," she continued, fighting back tears, "I can't concentrate on my studies, and if I don't concentrate, I will fail and have to go home." In Angola, as in so many countries suffering the effects of war, the danger was terrifying, but at least it was easy for the student to name, and there was no suggestion by anyone that she or her family bore the responsibility for the traumatic situation. But in the U.S., the land of plenty, the land of equal opportunity, if students' home neighborhoods are under siege, they are surrounded by ambivalent messages about who is to blame for that situation and the worthiness of character and intelligence of those who are unable to escape it, all of which creates anger, confusion, and guilt, however undeserved.

Academic writing and academic success in general are thus more problematic for involuntary minority students—especially when complicated by cultural differences, which may be evident even if a group has been resident in North America for some time. For example, Hispanic and Native American groups, which have been rejected by mainstream culture and maintain a strongly defined sense of difference from it, may value the same ways of understanding the world and expressing themselves in it that loosely characterize other world majority students: subtle, holistic, or contextual communication strategies, collectivist ideas of evidence, a learning style that absorbs rather than openly questions, and a valuing of ancient wisdom and the authority of teachers and texts. In combination, these cultural differences can cause at least some involuntary minority students to resist taking on an "academic" voice out of a real confusion about how they are expected to think about knowledge and express themselves in the university.

But African American students are different. Highly individualistic, even more straightforward than many mainstream students, with a questioning, critical outlook (e.g., Kochman 1981), African Americans do not see the characteristics of U.S. academic style as strange, or impolite, or simplistic the way other world majority students sometimes do. Getting the main idea in at the beginning of an essay, making clear and obvious connections, stating an original thesis or a strong personal opinion all seem as reasonable to African American students as to U.S. mainstream students. The reasons for this "western" orientation are complex, because African American communicative style retains many important linguistic and cultural connections with Africa. But those who know both African and African American communities well, or who come from one and observe the other, are struck immediately by some clear differences between the two cultural styles.

The most obvious difference is the directness of the African American "neighborhood style,"[14] in contrast to the African preference for subtlety. In the classroom, many African Americans are animated and personal and can be challenging to the point of confrontation, silencing white students when their numbers reach critical mass (about four African Americans out of a class of sixteen, in my experience), while African students are apt to keep silent for a long time in a discussion, or to wait until their ideas are asked for directly, even then taking their time to compose a careful, reflective response. Though African American style contains many indirect elements (for example, the avoidance of direct questions, the humorous insult by insinuation or "signifying," the use of parable and metaphor, and the ambiguity and double entendre used so often for protection and in-group communication in the days of slavery),[15] these forms of indirection do not seem to have the same effect on African American students' writing as do the indirect communication strategies used by other world majority cultures.

One of the reasons may be linguistic. As mentioned in Chapter 2, both the grammar and vocabulary of many languages encourage the expression of multiple forms of indirection—intentionally vague or abstract words, blurred verb tenses, different varieties of language to indicate the status of speaker and audience, and so on—while English is more suited to precision and directness. Thus the first languages of many world majority students, in combination with the polite and sophisticated indirection taught by their cultures, affect them at a deeper level, perhaps, than culture alone. African Americans, on the other hand, were forced to abandon their original languages and begin to speak English soon after their arrival, a survival strategy that may have affected their cultural communication style and world view as well.

Another clear difference between African American and African styles is the strong sense of individualism in the African American community, as evidenced by the diversity of opinion and the strong and obvious differences in personal style and expression. Africans, on the other hand, with their collectivist orientation, may be very guarded about giving a personal opinion and if pressed may give an enigmatic response or advance the general opinion of the group, which, as we have seen, may be quite different from what the individual really thinks. Certainly collectivist qualities survive and thrive in the African American community today: call and response rituals found in informal verbal play and in black church rhetoric, frequent calls for unity by student and community leaders, the playing down of differences of opinion in the presence of whites. Yet these aspects of African American culture are a far cry from the collectivism of Africa with its emphasis on spiritual holism and the preservation of harmony within the group, the social relationships and family allegiances that are the essence of African humanism: "I am because you are; you are because we are."[16]

Because African communicative style—at least those aspects of the style that seem to affect academic writing—is backgrounded within African American culture, African American college students do not experience the same clash of world view that affects so many students from other world majority cultures. While instructors may find a preference for narrative and concrete detail in some African American student writing that mirrors the pronounced and well-developed oral styles of black culture—styles expressed in the church, within the family, in political speeches, and with friends in the neighborhood— the underlying communicative characteristics of African American culture are not significantly different from the style that the university understands: one that is naturally straightforward, explicit, "logical," opinionated, and clear. What is standing in the way of African American students' success is not a confusion about how to think and express themselves in ways that are considered logical and sophisticated in U.S. culture, but rather the bizarre terms of their incorporation into mainstream society—terms that some students feel they must accept and ignore and fight all at the same time.[17]

One of the strangest, most contradictory papers I've ever seen was written by an African American freshman, perfectly at home with me in the library of a dorm where I was installed one evening ready to help students with their writing, not at all nervous or emotional as she read aloud page one, an angry tirade against white students "who come snooping around the Angela Davis lounge, looking at us as if we are some kind of tropical fish." The stance was so militantly antiwhite that I was silenced, not daring to suggest difficulties I was having with her reasoning or the resistance she would feel from her mostly white audience, the students in her first-year composition class.

But at the beginning of page two, the voice changed completely. Without warning, with no transition whatsoever, here was a description of the same dorm, where white students and students of color "get along like a happy family." *"We have learned words in each other's languages,"* Beth wrote, *"we have started going out for different ethnic foods."* It was the "we" that sounded so strange, so incongruously inclusive compared with the angry "us" and "them" of page one. Now the voice was calm and happy and reasonable, as if the world were perfect and everyone got along fine. And then at the end of the paper, a third voice emerged, one somewhat harder to define, again without transition, without warning. I remarked on this, and Beth smiled, and said yes, she knew it sounded disconnected. And although she was not sure why she began telling me this story, not completely sure of the connection between the disjointed paper and her life, she began, tentative but sincere:

"I grew up in a white suburb. I had never heard of welfare, or food stamps, or drugs. I didn't know those things existed. I had never even heard of a place where families didn't have swimming pools. And then, when I was thirteen, my parents got divorced, and we moved with my mother to a row house in Detroit. Suddenly I was going to an all-black high school, and kids were attacking me for 'acting white.' That's when I understood the experience of blacks in America."

"You mean *some* blacks in America," I said, smiling at her.

"I mean blacks in America," she repeated quietly.

"Mm. So that accounts for the anger in the first part of the paper, right?"

"Right," she said.

"But then here is this all-inclusive voice talking about 'we.' "

"I know. That's why I said at the beginning of my paper that I am more confused this semester than I have ever been in my life. Who am I? Who do I hold allegiance to? One moment I am with the militant students in the lounge, the next I am sitting in an all-white classroom, feeling perfectly fine."

As she tells me this, I realize that not until now has she stood back and looked at the situation from the outside; she had been too involved, too enmeshed in the confusing, shifting identities. The voices in the paper were her voices, but there was no outside narrator, no one to say "This is *me* at this moment, and this is *me* the next." She only half recognizes that these stances are opposing.

I draw some stick figures in the margin of her draft. "Here you are as a child, with your swimming pool," I say in explanation. "Here's your house in Detroit, and now here you are at the university."

I draw a bridge between the pool and the row house.

Beth looks at my scribbles for a long time. "Yes," she says finally, "that's what I have to do to get this paper to make sense. I have to figure out how to get across that bridge."[18]

Though idealists may still dream of a world free of prejudice, black leaders today have little hope of reforming mainstream society. "Racism will always be with us," says Bebe Moore Campbell. "We must stop asking America to love us and start to love ourselves." But I am not so pessimistic, for I believe that most racism in U.S. university classrooms today is born not of hatred, but of habit. Most mainstream teachers and students, I am convinced, sincerely believe they are free of bias and do not see the effects of even their most blatant actions and remarks. This condition does not have to remain chronic, however; the sooner we unearth our unexamined assumptions and unnecessary fears, the sooner we will eradicate the unnatural division between those who achieve and partake and those who do not.

Although changing our habitual ways of thinking will be difficult, there are nevertheless some simple, concrete steps that institutions and mainstream instructors can take to help African American and other involuntary minority students feel more at ease, even in the unwelcoming climate of the university. Claude Steele advises that universities stop labeling black students "at risk," for this confirms their worst fears. "Challenge these students academically, make them feel valued, avoid programs that segregate, and present black culture as part of the mainstream curriculum," he suggests (Magner 1992, A5).

With students like Joella, who do not dare to imagine themselves as the capable individuals they are, instructors need to demonstrate an understanding and appreciation of their cultural heritage and styles of expression,[19] at the same time challenging them to meet the highest standards for educational excellence in mainstream society, the standards we would set for our own children. A high achiever like Kendra, whose idealism was destroyed at a vulnerable age, needs to be given the chance to work out her emotional pain in her writing, even if her argument doesn't quite come clear. And if we catch a student like Wayne, the football player, before it's too late, we can challenge his competitive spirit instead of letting him slide by on the strength of his contributions to discussion, his reasonableness, his "good enough" compositions, his "silly" surface errors, even if we're sure he'll make a million bucks in the NFL and hire press agents to do his reading and writing for him.

But more than any of this, mainstream instructors need to join faculty members of color in their work with mainstream students—or with any students—who are contributing to the "acceptable" level of racism in the classroom and in the wider society. We need to work delicately, resisting the urge to hand them a ready-made analysis, or to tell them which are appropriate thoughts and ideas and which are not. How we decide to proceed is personal; taboo subjects like this one are unpredictable and tend to resist lesson plans and models. All we can do is be honest and share our experiences with each other. This is one of my attempts, one day . . .

A student comes into Writing Workshop, looking for "either help with transitions or ways to dig deeper into my subject."

"What's your subject?" I ask him.

"My experience with racism," he replies mildly.

I take a good look at him; he is white, like me, good-hearted, smiling, sincere. "Digging deeper is more interesting," I tell him.

He laughs and says, "All right. I don't really know what digging deeper means, but why not?" He sits down and hands me his paper. "It was pretty simple, actually," he says. "I was in Japan, in the service, and I got kicked out of a few bars because of my race. Not kicked out, actually. I hadn't even gotten in. There was a bouncer standing at the door, shouting at me. I was pretty clear he didn't want me in there, but I never really understood why."

"So you've told this story in your paper?"

"Yeah," he says, "and I've told a couple other stories too. Back in the States I went out with a Korean girl once, and her parents were very cold to me. I couldn't figure it out, because parents, well, parents *like* me." He shrugs and smiles at me a little self-consciously, and for an instant, I could see him at my door, waiting for my daughter, and yes, I agreed, I would like him. He is open, easy with words.

"But my problem in this paper is that I just tell these stories. They're just strung together, one after another. I don't know how to make the paper flow."

"It'll start to flow when you dig deeper," I tell him. "What's your theory? How do you suppose these people saw you?"

Silence. I look at him. He hasn't a clue. His face does not show any hurt, not even a trace of irritation with the way people have reacted to him. He's not even really curious. It just happened, and now he has to write this paper. Is it possible that he hasn't been touched by the experience?

The student glances at his watch. "I'd like you to take a look at my paper," he reminds me. "You'll see how I just string these stories together. Maybe you can help me come up with some transitions."

I read through his paper. It's true—it's just a collection of incidents related one after another without comment. "What are you trying to say with these stories?" I ask him.

He looks at me blankly and shakes his head.

"Well, let's see. There's something about yourself as a target. And you've got another kind of story here too," I tell him, and I read aloud what he has written about a friend who keeps quoting him the biblical injunctions against intermarriage. "What do you make of this?"

"Oh, he's not racist," the student assures me, guessing where I'm headed. "He has friends of many races. He even told me he would go out with someone of another race if he wanted to."

"Do you see a bit of a contradiction there?"

The student looks at me as if he doesn't understand my question. No, it seems logical to him. I tell him that it is probably impossible to grow up in this society without taking on its values. He nods, agreeable. I ask him if he might be a little racist himself. He is not offended by my question. I see him looking inward briefly, as if checking to see if he were hungry. "No," he says, "I'm not racist." I don't argue with him. I sit listening, thinking, conscious that the half-hour has nearly passed and we have not come up with a way to improve his paper.

"Do you see any racism in our society at all?" I ask him.

"Not really," he replies.

"What was your high school like? Did you come from a mixed community?"

"No," he says, "I come from a small town where there were no blacks or anything, but when I went into the service, people of all races were thrown together and everyone was treated like a piece of garbage, so we developed some solidarity."

I laugh, and tell him a little about my own experience going to an "integrated" high school in the 1950s, and how mixed couples hadn't been allowed at the prom.

"You know what it was like back then, so you can see it," he says. "But I can't."

"A longer view helps sometimes," I say, "but there are some things I have noticed only recently."

"Like what?" he asks, interested.

"Like the fact that even the most liberal people in the most liberal communities tolerate a certain 'acceptable' level of racism."

"So tell me, how did you come to that conclusion?" He is leaning forward, very interested now. I look inward, and remember Africa, remember the frank, open faces of people who do not have to apologize for who they are. I remember traveling upcountry with my project director, remember his warm laugh, his skin the rich brown of the hills and rivers, his startling green eyes; I remember my desire. I feel the sting, again, as I realize how this would look back home—and worse, how this would look even to me, the liberal, back home.

But I do not tell him any of these things. "This is *your* paper," I say, taking on the insufferable, chiding tone of a teacher who had been touched a little too personally by a student's questioning. "We have to get at what *you* think about all this." The student sighs. He is no closer to understanding.

I ask him why some blacks straighten their hair. He says he doesn't know. Probably has something to do with wanting to be like white people.

"Why would they want to do that?"

"Maybe to get access to power," he speculates.

"But if they had straight hair, would they really look like white people?"

"No," he admits.

"Well then, what's behind it?" He is stumped. I sigh a little. I'm going to have to be more graphic. "Think of the worst things whites have said about the features of people of other races." He thinks. He cannot come up with anything. "Slant eyes? Thick lips? Frizzy hair? Dirty skin?" I am very uncomfortable saying these ugly things that are so familiar, yet so denied. The student's expression changes ever so slightly in recognition.

"Well, yes," he concedes. "Maybe there is some of that in our society. But not in me. Not in anybody I know. Maybe I'm not attracted to darker-skinned girls, but that's only because I like a certain type. I don't especially like blond, blue-eyed girls either." I smile, suddenly conscious of my own blond hair. He goes on, oblivious of his faux pas. "It's not a matter of prejudice," he insists. "It's just preference. There's no reason behind it."

I ask him if he has ever heard of Frantz Fanon. He's a famous author, I tell him, a black psychiatrist from the Caribbean, and if he reads him, he will feel uncomfortable. I search his face when I say this, looking for signs of resistance, but I see only an open, interested expression. I ask him if he has some time over the weekend. Yes, he is willing to read, willing to explore. I write down "Black Skin, White Masks," on the student's paper—the only marks I have made on it during our half hour together—and hand it back to him.

The student sits there, looking at his paper, suddenly overwhelmed by what I am asking him to do. This is going to be more work than he realized, rewriting this paper. "It's not a writing problem you're having," I tell him. "It's not a problem with transitions. It's the problem of getting deeper into the subject, which means addressing a question, the question you keep asking: Why? Why are people in this world racist towards me? Or towards anybody?"

The student is nodding now. He is getting the idea. But one thing is still bothering him. "How am I going to get an *A* on my paper if I have to do all this, and I still might not come up with any answers?" Ah yes, the university, intervening in education. I assure him that making even a little progress on the questions will make it a better paper. He puts on his coat, shaking his head a little.

"Well," he says, "at least now I know what "digging deeper" means. "Yeah," I say, "I think you do." I am smiling, but my heart is tired.

7 Helping World Majority Students Make Sense of University Expectations

When academics argue about multiculturalism, they form predictable battle lines. On one side are those who would change the university, dispensing with the white male literary canon, adding more histories and literatures of maligned or ignored peoples, introducing research styles and purposes that include new voices and points of view. On the other side are those who would leave the university alone and change the students instead, providing them with the courses, the research opportunities, the quality time with faculty, even remedial help if necessary, in order to help them meet what they consider to be "world class" standards.

Each side sees the other as repressive. According to those who would change the university, requiring students to conform to dominant ways of thinking and of expressing ideas upholds a social order that allows ethnocentrism and racism to flourish. And according to those who would change the students, opening up the university to other styles and standards of excellence would create an even more elitist system in which those who chose western-traditional courses and methods would learn rigorously and move to the top, while those who did not would remain marginal.

Because this dispute has become so divisive and contentious, whenever I talk about "the problem" as I have framed it in this book—that world majority students are misjudged at the U.S. university because of cultural differences in communication style and world view—faculty members want to know where I stand. "So what should we do?" they ask. "Should we open up the university to a plurality of communication styles and ideas about knowledge, or should we help world majority students conform to our standards?"

If I were consistent, I would have to say, "Let's change the university." Given what I've said about the disabling effects of ethnocentrism and racism, and given my belief that communication styles and world views should be seen as different, rather than "good" or "poor," "world class" or "marginal," it would seem obvious that the university needs major reform, from its institutional goals to course offerings, to assessment criteria, to curricula, to assignments, to classroom and conferencing practices, all the way down to comments on individual students' papers.

But students cannot wait for change. They are here, trying to get along in the system, and they know they need to understand it in order to succeed. "I accepted that I would have to learn what western faculty have to offer when I came here, when I sat down in class to learn from them," says Ali, a graduate student from Somalia. "So I have to try hard to meet their requirements. Because what I'm here for is to get what they have. They will certify that I have graduated. If I don't want it that way, then I shouldn't be here in the first place. So I just want to know what the rules are. I just want to know how things are operating, what's considered good writing and what's considered bad writing. Then I can try to conform to that, so I can graduate, so I can achieve my objectives here."

"We can't expect the university to change," Kamala tells me in a cynical and uncharacteristically direct moment. "Professors have tenure. They have no reason to adjust their thinking." "We come from so many different cultures," adds Jean-Claude, trying to smooth over her criticism. "Faculty can't learn about them all. I was surprised to find that many of my professors have never been abroad, even for a short time. It's hard to understand the way another culture thinks unless you spend time in the country and learn the language."

But while these students find it impractical to change the system, they are not completely content with the status quo. "If this culture demands foreign students to be different," says Surya, "can't foreign students demand this culture to be different, a little bit, so we can come to a point were we can communicate with each other? I don't want to say that we don't have to change; I don't have to remain the way I was in my country, that's kind of an arrogant position. But why can't people here, even professors, try to be different? Why can't they accept the styles the students bring with them, and also educate themselves so that they can understand others?"

As I listen to these students, I realize that we must do both—change the students and change the university—even if it seems contradictory, even if doing so seems to support ethnocentrism at the same time we try to dismantle it. First, we need to help students cope within the system as it exists, with all its imperfections. If we do this in the way I will suggest, by talking explicitly about cultural differences when we have determined it to be appropriate, we will at least be acknowledging, to students and to ourselves, that other reasonable, logical ways of seeing the world exist and are of interest to U.S. faculty. This in itself would be an enormous step forward for the university, given its entrenched and almost willful ignorance of other points of view.

Secondly, we need to find ways, as Surya suggests, to educate ourselves so that we can understand others. Not only would this be more respectful to the rest of the world, it is also, in his view, more realistic. "The way I see it, the university is saying, 'You are here, so you have to accept our system.' We do understand that, and we have to be pretty much adjustable to that. But the thing is, how far can we go with it? How much can we change in a period of two or three years? So if both the students and the university would change, at least somewhat, we wouldn't have to wrestle with the level of frustration that we have, thinking that we have to become so absolutely different. Because how can we do this? What is the process, what is the way we can change so radically here so that we can be accepted, so that we can gain recognition? That's where the self-esteem, the self-confidence comes from. Foreign students have been getting recognition for the ways they have been thinking and communicating and writing in their previous settings. And all of a sudden they lose all that. You can't imagine what happens to these people! They become very irritated. Very much miserable."

In the light of these comments from students themselves, who, after all, are the ones we are trying to help, I will suggest some ways that I have been using to work with undergraduate and graduate students who I see in class, or in weekly conferences over the intensive seven-week half-term, or in a one-shot half-hour conference in Writing Workshop. These ways of talking with students (which I have illustrated through stories in previous chapters) seem to work, at least some of the time, both for the students and for myself. For when I say that these suggestions "work," it means two things to me: first, that they help students change their writing—their styles and their entire approach, sometimes quickly, sometimes through a long period of struggle. Second, talking with students about cultural influences on their writing means that I must be constantly aware of these influences, constantly demonstrating to students that I understand—or want to understand—where they are coming from. Because of this demand for openness on my part, these conversations "work" on me as well, reminding me constantly of what it is like to experience the world differently. And once I understand that, I can begin to see ways to help students adjust their styles to their new audience without completely losing themselves. I can begin to see ways of experimenting with assignments, even for mainstream students, assignments that call for more subtlety or metaphor or storytelling and less explicit analysis or writing that is more digressive than is usually acceptable in the university context, which I might accompany with an explanation of the purpose of this communication style and its cultural and intellectual origins. I can begin to talk with other faculty members, especially with those who are trying to promote "critical thinking," about how I am working with our multicultural population, and I can suggest, whenever I have the opportunity, that our emphasis on an explicit, challenging, academic style has an important cultural component. I can help committees rethink assessment criteria or dissertation requirements. I can help peer tutors see beyond the editing of surface errors on second-language students' papers. I can do all this once I have a clear idea of what it is like to think and express one's self differently, once I am convinced— just as I want my world majority students to be convinced—that there is more than one way of understanding the world. And I can gain confidence in these kinds of conversations through practice, by working with students as they come into my office one by one.

When to Talk to World Majority Students about Cultural Differences

As previous chapters suggest, the most effective way I have found to help world majority students reach their U.S. university audience is to talk with them about cultural differences in styles of communicating, thinking, and understanding the world. This almost invariably eases students' tension and catches their interest, especially when you explain how U.S. communicative style is connected with our ideas about "good writing."

But it would be a mistake to plunge into this discussion too quickly, for as we have seen, talking about cultural differences can have touchy political implications. Because of the pervasive idea that western communication styles and ideas of "analysis" and "critical thinking" are somehow superior to those of other cultures (or that they might even represent "higher order" thinking), students need to feel very certain that you are not criticizing their abilities or their upbringing before they will talk with you about possible differences in their ways of thinking and writing.

And even when students trust you, it would not be a good idea to assume that anyone who comes from abroad or, worse, anyone whose last name is Wong or Das Gupta or Hernandez must have a particular writing or thinking style, or must be affected by cultural differences to the same degree or in the same way as other world majority students, or even at all. There are so many variations in students' histories, so many factors in each one's family and educational background, not to mention the confounding effects of personality, gender, and life experiences that can accentuate or mute the effects of culture.

When we work with individual students, then, it is important to approach gradually the issue of how cultural differences might be influencing their writing. I try to get some idea about this by taking the time for some conversation the first time I see them. While we are talking, I try to listen not only to what students are saying, but also for accent, grammar, syntax, vocabulary, and appropriate slang. I might begin by asking where they are from and how long they've been in the U.S. If I find they have just come, I will ask if they are doing okay—feeling comfortable or a little homesick—and perhaps establish any connections or special interest I might have in their home country or culture: "Oh, Hong Kong! I've worked with quite a few students from there." "You're from Tokyo? What university did you transfer from?" "Belize—I'm ashamed to say I don't know where that is. Can you help me out?" "São Tomé! I don't think I've ever met someone from there. Your first language is Portuguese, then, is that right?"

If the student has lived in the U.S. awhile, I ask if she had been placed in ESL classes in elementary or high school, how long she stayed in them, and what she thought of them. I might ask how she works on her spoken English most effectively (friends? family? TV? formal study?) and what her living situation is on campus (living with family members or friends who speak her first language? rooming with an American or international student who doesn't?). If the student is a newcomer, I usually give some encouragement at this point to make friends and interact more with students from other cultures in order to improve her spoken English more rapidly—at which the student invariably smiles and shyly agrees, for this kind of immersion at the level of the social support system is difficult for most foreign students, just as it is for U.S. students when they go abroad. I never write anything down during this brief conversation, for I want the interview to be taken for what it is—friendly, caring, and personal, rather than some kind of bureaucratic fulfillment of job assignments or, worse, information that the student suspects might end up in a permanent file.

If I expect to work with a student for some time, I also ask about future goals. Does this first-year student from Taiwan plan to return to her country after four years or does she hope to stay on in the U.S. to study medicine or social work? Does this U.S. Spanish speaker, transferring here from a two-year college, plan to do youth outreach work in the Latino community or is he applying for the business school? This information will help give me an idea of how the student intends to use not only the English language, but the ways of thinking and communicating that are valued by the U.S. university. I do this *not* to set goals for the student or to decide what level of skill in academic writing is appropriate (which would be an egregious abuse of power), but I will be more urgent in my advice about change if, for example, a student wants to study U.S. law than if she intends to return to Korea to work in her country's ministry of education.

All this conversation—which should never be put to the student as a list of questions, but should develop naturally, according to your own interests and what the student feels comfortable telling you—will help you determine if the student's home culture might be affecting the writing in the U.S. context. There is a good chance that culture will be a factor if any of the following conditions apply: (a) the student is a newcomer—even if he seems to be very "western" in dress, English ability, and background; (b) the student has been in the U.S. for some time—three years or more—and is still having trouble with oral English or makes many grammar mistakes in writing; or (c) if the student speaks English relatively well, but describes his home as "very traditional" and continues to speak the maternal language with family.

On the other hand, if the student has few or no oral language difficulties, has many English-speaking friends, has been in the U.S. for some time or was born here, or has led a very "western" style of family life in her home country, her writing, communicative style, and general intellectual outlook may be similar to that of U.S. mainstream students. If I feel this is the case, I don't mention cultural differences at all, but give the student the same advice about writing (and make the same assumptions about how it will be understood) as I would give any U.S. mainstream or African American student. I also might refrain from mentioning cultural difference if the student appears to devalue or dismiss the maternal language and culture, which nowadays is more common among students from involuntary minority backgrounds than among students from abroad, but is also sometimes true of members of elite families in some former British colonies such as Singapore or Sri Lanka; students from these backgrounds may speak only English and see themselves as primarily "western" in orientation and may even at times look down on others in their country who are not as "westernized" or who do not speak English as flawlessly as they do. This is a touchy situation; culture may indeed be affecting the writing, but mentioning it may lead students to think you are singling them out in order to accentuate what they see as their only too obvious weaknesses. And although it hurts to see students disparage their own roots (it seems to me a way of belittling themselves), I usually do not give advice to these students about valuing their first language and culture. After all, have I searched out my own German, Irish, and Scottish roots, learned their languages, appreciated their customs? No, I haven't had much interest in this idea. My grandparents and great-grandparents disappeared into the melting pot long ago.

Once I have a sense of the degree to which cultural differences affect individual students' writing, I'm ready to take a look at the papers they have brought me, usually by reading them out loud or having the students do so, stopping them where I am confused, and talking about why I'm having a problem getting the drift of what they want to say. Unless the students insist that surface errors are the only thing I should look at, I disregard most errors in grammar or vocabulary the first time through the paper, though I occasionally suggest a different word or phrase to help my understanding. I let the students know I am doing this and assure them that we will work on grammar later, after we have looked at the deeper features of organization and style. If the paper comes from outside my class, I ask about any comments the students might have gotten from other instructors and listen for any sense of confusion or discouragement over feedback received on organization, style, or interpretation of the assignment. I especially look for signs that the students are having difficulty accepting advice or criticism concerning culturally based components of academic writing: coming to the point sooner, making the point clearer, making explicit transitions between ideas, being more precise or literal in the use of words, referencing specific quotes or paraphrases, avoiding overgeneralization, doing explicit analysis, tying analysis to narrative or example, removing "irrelevant" material, and giving an opinion or coming up with an "original" or independent thesis.

Of course, as I have mentioned before, all these problems may occur with U.S. mainstream writers as well. But unlike U.S. mainstream students, who understand the logic behind such feedback, whether we are irritated ("your point?") or more respectful ("I don't understand what you are trying to say here"), world majority students may be quite confused about why these "improvements" are so important or may be having more difficulty carrying them out than they—or their instructors—think they should be. Once I feel confident—from discovering the students' background, noticing their reaction to instructor feedback, and looking at the paper itself—that cultural differences are affecting the writing in important ways, I am ready to talk about the differences themselves.

Making the Main Point Clear

If the point of the piece is unclear to me because of a digressive style
or vague, abstract language, or a lack of specific examples or excessive
preliminaries or extraneous material unrelated to the main idea, or if
I am expecting the paper to answer a question that it does not in fact
address, I begin by saying that I understand there are cultural differences in communication styles and that I realize that, in some cultures,
being too direct might seem simplistic or even impolite. Sometimes I
tell students that they may have heard that being indirect or vague
or digressive means the writing isn't "good" and that I don't necessarily
agree with that. I tell them that I believe that communication style is
relative and that how we talk or write is determined by what the
audience expects or needs. In most cultures, the audience expects not
to be hit over the head with the point right at the beginning. But here
in the U.S., I tell them, we do. Just as they have been taught that
respecting readers or listeners means not telling them what they can
figure out for themselves, respecting the audience in the western
academic context means making things so explicit and precise that
they can follow the argument without any effort at all.

To illustrate this, I might say—especially to newcomers—that they
probably have noticed how direct Americans are, how quickly everything is done here, how people seem to have no time to really get to
know each other. I might even play this up a little at the expense of
U.S. culture: "Remember, time is money!" I say, a maxim that people
around the world always seem to associate with the U.S. I might also
tell them they need to talk to Americans the way they talk to their
computer, spelling everything out in great detail and with great
precision: one imperfect connection, one wrong command, and you'll
lose us! By this time I usually have them laughing, and we can now
more easily look at their writing and try to define the main point a
little more clearly without any sense of shame on their part.

These students have not, for the most part, made the connection
between writing and the communicative style that they have been
learning from the time they were very small—the combination of body
language, vocabulary, phrasing, tone, voice, and content that is considered well mannered and intellectually appropriate in their own
cultural context. Even if they do know, for example, that Asians often
express themselves in a more indirect or circular way than westerners,
they may be feeling a little ashamed about not being straight-line
thinkers, a mode that they know is considered smart, logical, cost-

effective, and the only way to get ahead by legions of ethnocentric Americans.

It's also important to remember that most students from abroad have studied English grammar and vocabulary longer than they'd like to remember, and most of them have had explicit, basic instruction on how to put a paragraph together. They know there is supposed to be a "topic sentence" or main point, which is generally followed by development or elaboration with relevant examples, and that each paragraph is supposed to be connected to the next by some kind of transition. If they have passed the TOEFL (Test of English as a Foreign Language), the English entrance exam for international college students, it means that they have succeeded in constructing deductive paragraphs, at least in very short essays some of the time. But for the most part, world majority students have never understood *why* a paragraph in English needs to be structured so precisely, except that it is "the right way," or a "good" or "clear" or "coherent" paragraph, which, pasted together with four other similarly structured paragraphs, becomes the famous five-paragraph essay, which is also "clear" and "coherent" but which, stylistically, is not particularly interesting or elegant, or convincing, from their point of view.

"*Over the last decade, an average of at least one country a year has abolished capital punishment, declaring its respect for human life,*" writes a Japanese student. "*Nevertheless in the United States, the condemnations of capital punishment are still pronounced by some states.*" Keiko knows how to begin clearly, giving the reader a good idea of what the essay is about, and hinting, not too subtly, at the stance she intends to take. She knows she is supposed to connect her thoughts with transitions and she chooses an appropriate one to do so. But what she doesn't realize is how strange it sounds to a U.S. audience when she leaves out the explicit information between those two thoughts: that the U.S. has lagged behind other countries in abolishing capital punishment, which is the reason those condemnations are still heard in some states. I talk with her about this, making my own explicit connections between audience needs and culture.

"You've left out a piece of information, I think, that's really important for people who need to have everything spelled out to them," I tell her. "You need to say the obvious here, that in the U.S. there are some states that still execute prisoners. Even if it sounds a little stupid, you need to take your readers by the hand and walk them through the argument."

After revising this piece many times according to my suggestions about explicitness, Keiko's first paragraph reads:

> *Over the last decade, many countries have abolished capital punish-*
> *ment, declaring respect for human life. Nevertheless in the United*
> *States, some states still believe in capital punishment and more than*
> *dozens of prisoners are executed every year despite the urgent effort*
> *by citizens to abolish this cold-blooded official killing. In times when*
> *human rights all over the world are affirmed, why do these states*
> *punish prisoners with death?*

At the end of the seven-week course, Keiko writes her reflections on
the experience of learning to write for a U.S. audience:

> *Another thing that made me crazy was that I had to write everything*
> *I wanted to say so that readers could understand the point. In Japanese*
> *writing we do not write everything we want to say. Writers can give*
> *readers some ideas or hints but not clear answers. Although these*
> *differences are interesting, it's really hard for me to do well in this*
> *class because of them. But after all, it was kind of fun to write in a*
> *different way of thinking.*

"Why do more Americans die?" This is the third or fourth time that
Jong, a first-year Korean student, has tried to state his thesis at the
opening of a five-page argument on a current issue in the media. Jong
is an older student; he already has a degree in economics but has
come back for a second bachelor's in computer science, which he has
decided will be more practical. Even after successfully completing four
years at a U.S. university, he scored in the lowest 12 percent of all
entering students on the essay entrance exam and was placed, along
with fifteen other embarrassed freshmen, in my introductory class in
academic argument. Jong and I have already had a number of discussions about cultural tendencies toward directness and indirectness,
and he has become quite interested in the idea. He tells me he is just
beginning to realize the connection between U.S. academic style and
a more "Americanized" version of himself that he sees on the horizon,
one who is "aggressive and direct." He is not sure he likes this vision.

"Why do more Americans die? More than who, Jong? Die of what?
What's this paper about?"

Jong smiles and shakes his head. "I am still not specific enough,"
he says, chiding himself.

"You're hinting at something, and that's intriguing. But your audience will be confused if you don't tell them more at the beginning.
You've probably noticed that Americans don't like to wait, right?"

Jong smiles and looks down at his paper. "That's true," he says.

"We don't have the patience to be led gradually to understand what
your topic is. What is it, by the way?"

"Gun control," says Jong.

"Gun control!" I repeat in mock surprise.

Jong laughs. "I wanted to compare statistics on deaths from gunshot wounds in the U.S. and Canada."

"Oh, so more Americans die than Canadians? Why didn't you say so?"

"So my thesis should be, "Why do more Americans die than Canadians from gunshot wounds?"

"Is that what the paper is about?"

"Hm. That's interesting." Jong is silent, thinking. "I think there's more in the paper than that," he says, nodding.

"So it's not only a comparison of those two countries?"

Jong thinks long and hard. "I think it's a paper about my opinion about gun control."

"So what *is* your opinion?"

"Hm," says Jong thoughtfully. "That's interesting."

Digressive or "Irrelevant" Material

Peter, a Chinese American freshman, comes to me with a paper on eastern approaches to medicine. In talking with him, I have decided that he is integrated enough into U.S. society that I probably won't see much in the way of cultural differences in his writing. He was born here, he has not a trace of an accent, he is enrolled in a multicultural living and learning program at the university, and he seems completely at ease answering my rapid-fire questions about the course, the instructor, and the curriculum they have covered so far. As I begin reading his paper, my first impression seems to be confirmed; his thesis is up front and pretty clear, the gist of it being that eastern medicine should be taken seriously by the west because "it works." Evidence follows with a story of a man with a severe case of ulcerative colitis who recovered with the help of a Chinese herbal cure. So far, so good. But after these few pages the argument is abandoned and the rest of the paper is taken up with the history of eastern medicine and its many categories and types without any more reasons to believe it works and without any particular conclusions. Peter knows there is something not quite right about the way he has put the paper together, but he feels strongly that the history and typology need to be included in just this form. "I know it's digressive," he says. "And I want to do something about that. But I don't want to cut any of this—it's too important."

This to me is a clue—polite stubbornness about a form that doesn't quite work, or, in this case, stubbornness about a form that doesn't work at all. So instead of simply telling him what material is irrelevant to his argument and suggesting the kinds of specific evidence he should add instead, I ask him what he wants to say or demonstrate with the history and typology of eastern medicine. Right away, he gives me verbally the kind of direct, analytical statements that he has left out of his paper: "I've put in these details to show that eastern medicine has been around a long time, that it's been carefully studied, and that it works because it is based on careful observations of the patient's reactions. There is something intuitive about eastern medicine," he continues, "an understanding of subtlety, of balance. Such things cannot and are not tested scientifically. Careful observations of patients' reactions to herbs and other remedies, accumulated over thousands of years, have created this practice—not in a systematic sense, but through an accumulation of wisdom."

From the quick, concise way that Peter sums up this argument for me, it is clear that he feels at home with explicit analysis. But in his paper, instead of saying that a *reason* we should take eastern medicine seriously is that it has a long history, he has simply detailed the history and let the audience make the connection by themselves. Instead of saying that eastern medicine is based on unsystematic observation that nevertheless became increasingly complex, organized, and remarkably effective over the centuries, he has laid out the complicated typology and let the audience observe it and draw their own conclusions. I describe what I see him doing here and talk a little about cultural tendencies to indirectness and subtlety, drawing a parallel between what he's been telling me about the art of eastern medicine and the way he has written this passage, and, similarly, between the science of western medicine and the "scientific" preciseness and directness of western academic writing. This interests him enormously; he realizes that the digressiveness he has noticed about his writing has something to do with asking his audience to come to an intuitive understanding of what U.S. communicative style would make explicit or "analytical." Peter leaves my office with a glimpse of a new idea—a big idea— more important, perhaps, than any practical advice I could give him about getting rid of digressive or "irrelevant" material in his paper.

Compare and Contrast

A U.S. student whose parents come from India arrives with a paper comparing the purposes of fasting in Islam and Christianity. I scan the text; there is too much descriptive background on each religion without a careful focus on fasting and without a tight enough framework comprising specific points of comparison. I begin by saying that using this structure is indeed a valid way to write about fasting in two religions but that her audience will be expecting a more closely drawn comparison. I have not had time, with this student, to do any kind of interview, and except for a quick initial impression (English is flawless, no accent, seems similar in body language to U.S. mainstream eighteen- or nineteen-year-olds), I do not know how much her cultural background might be affecting her writing, if it is at all. But there is no harm in talking about the validity of different types of organization, stressing that different styles require different things of the reader, and that the indirect style she is using will be more difficult for her university audience to grasp. She seems to understand, right away, what I am getting at—which is rarely the case with a student strongly situated in another way of seeing the world.

When I work with a student who seems to be strongly influenced by an indirect style, I might first talk a little about cultural differences and then explain several ways of organizing a compare-and-contrast paper more explicitly. I might start by pulling out themes that the student has already identified and then asking questions leading to the discovery of an additional theme or two. Then I show the student visually, with a quick sketch, several different ways of comparing these themes. Sketches are cross-cultural; I always have a pad of paper handy to draw stick figures and diagrams that show the explicit relationships the student needs to draw with words. I mention that you can sometimes see the similarity between mathematics and writing in U.S. academic style if you replace ideas with symbols; for example, one way of organizing this compare-and-contrast paper would be to think about fasting in Islam and fasting in Christianity as two sets, I and C, with the same five or so themes in each set:

$$
\begin{array}{cc}
\mathbf{I} & \mathbf{C} \\
T_1 & T_1 \\
T_2 & T_2 \\
T_3 & T_3 \\
T_4 & T_4 \\
T_5 & T_5 \\
\end{array}
$$

Or, alternatively, you could think of each of the five themes as a set containing the ideas of the two religions:

T₁

I

C

T₂

I

C

Etc.

Undergraduates from abroad are often strong in math and will catch on quickly, once the ideas, grammar, and vocabulary are out of the way for the moment so that they can focus on organization. The next step is to model the explicit language they might use to talk about the ideas they are comparing: "While in Islam, fasting means X, in Christianity it means Y"; or "In Islam, fasting means X; on the other hand, in Christianity it means Y." I usually write these sentences out on paper for students to take home and use as models; they may understand this concept easily while we are talking about it, but then lose it when they start their next draft and become immersed again in the ideas and the language.

Linking U.S. academic style with math also helps students understand our expectation that writers make the relationships between ideas very explicit. When they use active verbs and conjunctions that show cause and effect, when they make sure that subjects can do what the verbs suggest they can, when they use transition words and expressions or pick up the language of the previous paragraph in the next, they are linking ideas in much the same way as they would link numbers with plus or minus signs or other mathematical symbols—and for much the same reason: to tell the reader directly how they intend the terms or ideas to be related to each other.

While working with students on constructing their papers a little more mathematically, I often emphasize that this rather mechanical way of presenting ideas might seem a little tedious to read, and that I realize it may leave out a great deal that could be more comfortably expressed within a looser or more digressive framework, or by letting the readers do more of the connection and interpretation themselves. Still, using this style is a successful way to communicate with instructors on a complex subject, I tell them, because it will always be obvious what the points of comparison are, and how and to what degree these points are similar and different—the kind of information the instructors value, in a form they are anticipating and can easily understand.

Critiquing Authorities

Because direct criticism is embarrassingly impolite or even politically dangerous in many cultures, expecting world majority students to feel at home critiquing the authors they read is somewhat unrealistic. This problem is often more evident at the graduate level than it is for undergraduates; first-year students from any culture often feel, quite rightly, that they don't have enough experience or information to evaluate critically what authorities in the field have said. By their junior or senior year, however, and certainly by the graduate level, we expect that they *do* know enough—at least enough to venture an analysis of how carefully a study was constructed, how significant are the results of an experiment, how logical a given theory is or how applicable in practice. But in cultures that are based on a stricter, more pervasive hierarchy, students feel—and *are*—subordinate longer; until they have credentials and status, their role is to accumulate information, not to critique it. "Maybe that's what Paulo Freire calls 'banking education,'" says a Brazilian graduate student. "That's what has social value in my culture—if a person shows they know lots of details. It's not so much what you do with that information that's important."

To help students take on a different role in U.S. culture with its more egalitarian assumptions, I sometimes suggest that students imagine themselves in a specific position of authority when they write. If for example, they are to critique the university's policy on multiculturalism, I might ask them to imagine they are a consultant on this issue reporting to a faculty committee; if they are supposed to mention the strengths and drawbacks of a social agency in the community, I might suggest that they assume the role of outside evaluator or social work supervisor called in to help the agency adopt specific policy measures to improve their services. Stressing that this is playacting and carefully defining both the role and the task can help students go beyond descriptions of policies and services into the less familiar area of frank, detailed critique.

Though many world majority students need encouragement to critique authorities, I have known others who take to it with unexpected zeal. Mohammed, a community activist from Indonesia who was used to attacking the ideologies of other political factions but not quibbling (as he saw it) with those who followed his own school of thought, looked forward to the increased freedom to criticize others in the U.S. context. "When I came to graduate school here, I thought, 'This is an ideal society; I will attack everybody!'" he told me. "So I began to strongly argue with all my professors in class. But soon I found that some I had counted as my friends became very distant. And then I realized that it's just like in my culture; people hurt, as human beings, when you argue with them directly."

Working with students like Mohammed can be difficult because, like many Americans who travel abroad, he does not easily distinguish the nuances of an unfamiliar culture. While he is trying to decide whether U.S. professors are either very sensitive, like he is, or completely immune to criticism, he may overlook an important idea: that academic argument is generally couched in relatively cool, objective language that focuses attention away from the person and onto the ideas being evaluated in order to get at "the truth," or at least at a smart, sensible way of looking at a topic, which, we believe, will further the cause of "science" or "reason." If Mohammed wants a deeper understanding of "how this culture thinks," he will need time— time with an understanding adviser, time observing presentations and critique in seminars and conferences, and plenty of opportunities to carry out his professors' expectations for "independent thought" and critical analysis in writing.

At the same time, if the faculty members who work with him want to understand why his writing seems to have so many difficulties— difficulties with emotional language, with insufficient evidence, with clear, direct statements of his own position—they need to understand a little more about why his way of expressing himself makes sense in the context of his culture. Indonesia is a land of incredible cultural and geographic diversity: more than three hundred ethnic groups, five major religions, and thousands of languages and dialects scattered over thirteen thousand islands. This diversity has contributed to the propensity of its people to identify themselves with factions and sects—and, Mohammed suggests, for its intellectuals to ally themselves with separate, often competing schools of thought. Though these groups may adopt a live-and-let-live philosophy or, at times, may critique each other openly, nevertheless, within each group, harmony and collectivist solidarity are valued over expressions of individual difference or quibbles over precise details of evidence. Thus, when Mohammed adopts a position he tends to adopt it wholesale; if he were to critique a major tenet of his own school of thought, it would be tantamount to declaring his allegiance to an opposing school. In fact, he told me, in Javanese culture, where drawing attention to yourself is considered childish, the accepted way to let your audience know your position is by allying yourself with a group; you need only take on the language of a particular faction and explain things as they do, and your position will be obvious.

Engaging students like Mohammed in conversation about why they present their topics the way they do, making the cultural expectation for direct critique clear, and providing opportunities for them to practice weighing and balancing the positions of different authors, "letting their views rub up against each other," as one of his professors put it, will be useful—especially if such opportunities are offered long before students take on major papers or writing for publication.

Plagiarism

A professor of art history comes to see me at the end of the semester, wanting to know if I have an official handout on plagiarism. As I search my files, I ask her what the problem is. "This student is a graduating senior," she tells me, "but there is no way he will pass my course. I've talked to him several times about plagiarism, so he knows what it means. But he continues to lift passages right out of the text. In other places, I can see where he's changing just a few of the words, thinking he can get away with it."

I look up at her; she's not angry, just stating the facts.

"Is this an international student?" I ask.

"Yes. Korean," says the instructor.

I close the file drawer. "I'll find you the handout if you like," I tell her. "But since you've already explained to him what he's doing wrong and he continues to do it, I don't think the definition and examples we've got here will help. This student comes from a system where the relationship between the student and the authority of teachers and texts is very different from what it is here. I don't think he's trying to get away with anything, I think he's just not as convinced as we are that his own words are more important than those of the author."

"He understands about individual ownership of ideas," the instructor says. "That seems quite clear to him."

"But the concept of the individual is different in our society than it is in his. In our culture, children are trained to think of themselves as separate individuals from the time they are born. We put our infants in separate beds, even in separate rooms away from their parents and siblings—something that people from many cultures find shocking, like a kind of child abuse. And as they grow up we set them apart from us in mechanical contraptions: walkers, highchairs, baby swings, playpens. We give them objects to play with instead of human hands to hold. They are separate individuals before they learn to walk. And we continue to reinforce this concept as they get older—on the playground, in the classroom, in family interactions. But in most cultures, children have grown up much more connected to other human beings, so it's hard for them to feel convinced that it is all that important to delineate whose ideas are whose and to sanction those who don't respect personal boundaries."

"I hadn't thought about that," says the instructor. "But then how do we evaluate such a student, especially when he's about to graduate? I don't know how it's possible that he has come so far in the university without coming up against this before."

"Students don't necessarily have to do a lot of writing during their four years here," I remind her. "It's possible to take courses that are evaluated by multiple-choice exams or short essay questions that just ask for facts. I recently worked with a dentist from the Middle East doing his master's in public health administration who was doing much the same thing as your student—changing the text only slightly and using enormous quotes from a single source rather than coming up with his own argument. His instructor had the same question, how to evaluate the student, especially after she understood that the misunderstanding was cultural. In the end, she gave him only a bit more leeway than the others, even though he was terribly nervous and dissatisfied with his grade. She says it's her responsibility to uphold the same standards for everyone. But she also says she feels lucky that she was once a foreign exchange student at a high school in the Philippines—it's given her an idea of what these students are going through."

"So what do you suggest I do?"

"There's no easy answer," I tell her. "I think it's best to look carefully at what he is doing on his papers that is really bothering you. If it's simply a matter of the number of words he has changed in his paraphrase, he can get help in fixing that relatively easily. But if you really want him to develop an independent argument, and what he is doing is stitching together pieces of text from various sources, that's a different matter. He won't be able to completely change the way he envisions the assignment in a few weeks at the end of the semester— and if he is like the dentist, he'll be so fed up that he won't want to, either. For a student who is more practically than theoretically inclined and who is about to return to a different cultural system, learning to view the individual differently and then translating that into academic writing might not be particularly relevant."

"This is complicated," says the instructor. "But I can see that, for my student at least, holding up his graduation probably isn't a reasonable solution to the plagiarism problem."

"Analysis" or "Critical Thinking"

"This is strictly descriptive material," says a terse note describing a Kenyan student's doctoral dissertation. "The author's perspective is almost non-existent. There is no attempt to discover why the educational system is as it is. The present system is not placed within the cultural context of the time. The brief history of Kenya does not help to explain the present structure or its curriculum."

This note to me, written by a professor who had agreed to find examples of "poor analysis" for my study, illustrates the failure of the system at its height: a mid-career doctoral student has put in four or five years of his life away from his home, family, and profession and has finally sent his dissertation to his committee for their approval. But he has gotten so little useful help along the way with writing and thinking in the U.S. university context that all his work is now being devalued; even if he does receive his degree, it will not be considered anywhere near "world class." This situation might have been avoided, years ago, if the faculty giving feedback on course papers and his advisers in the dissertation process had understood that his articulate, thorough, completely off-the-point style was culturally based rather than an embarrassing flaw in his preparation or "thinking process."

Talking about "analysis" with world majority students always involves talking about cultural expectations. As I have tried to show, this thing we call "critical thinking" or "analysis" has strong cultural components. It is more than just a set of writing and thinking techniques—it is a voice, a stance, a relationship with texts and authorities that is taught, both consciously and unconsciously, by family members, friends, teachers, the media, even the history of one's country. This is why "critical analysis" is so hard for faculty members to talk about; because it is learned intuitively it is easy to recognize, like a face or a personality, but it is not so easily defined and is not at all simple to explain to someone who has been brought up differently. Doing "critical analysis" involves the cultural expectation to write assertively—or "aggressively," as many world majority students experience it. It means making overt connections within and between sentences and paragraphs and finding words that show exact relationships between ideas, as is required in a low-context culture. It means noticing and seeing as important small differences in individual authors' personalities, styles, and "takes" on an intellectual problem. It means valuing separateness over harmony and quick, new solutions over lengthy, mature reflection. It means being so explicit that little is left to the imagination or to the interpretive powers of the audience. It means a kind of writing that can seem as boring, redundant, and rude to world majority students as their writing may seem obscure, or digressive, or overly descriptive, or disturbingly unoriginal to their U.S. professors.

But while cultural collisions always have the potential to produce shock or distaste, they also have inherent in them the power to enrich the way both the world majority and the western minority understand and experience the world. In many cultures around the world today, especially among the young, the influence of the west in intellectual matters as well as in popular culture is becoming more noticeable. There is a questioning of tradition, a more assertive tackling of practical and intellectual problems, a more determined attempt to break down oppressive hierarchies through education for empowerment in poverty-stricken communities[1] and grass-roots movements demanding multi-party democracies. And although the west is not nearly so open to the borrowing and merging of traditions, critics within our ranks are beginning to describe academic argument as too contentious, too limiting, lacking in beauty and inspiration. Western academics are realizing, too, that the ways we have been taught to analyze and reason provide only limited solutions to human problems; although we are proud of our tradition of individualism and self-reliance, at times we find ourselves longing for connection, for meaning, for a greater sense of community, for harmony. We would do well to learn from each other.

What does the university need to hear about multiculturalism? That there are ways to see and experience the world that most of us have never dreamed of, ways of creating and communicating knowledge that are vastly different from what we have long been convinced is "good writing," "good thinking," and "proper understanding." As teachers, we have an obligation to help world majority students find a voice at the university by explaining in respectful, knowledgeable ways how we expect them to think, investigate, and express themselves in the U.S. context. And if we listen closely to what they have to tell us, we will not only teach more competently but deepen the meaning of our own intellectual lives as well.

I know that listening to the world takes time. Becoming aware of the richness of each student's background, *feeling* how it is to think differently, surely this is impossible to do for each of the hundreds of students we see each year. But still, if we could just get to know one student from another culture in a meaningful way, in a way that surprises us, or confuses us, or forces us to think again about our assumptions . . .

Even just one . . .

Epilogue

Let me tell you one last story—the story of how I got to know Madelaine, a shy, determined student from Mali, West Africa, who was struggling with writing and with the expectations of the U.S. university. Let me tell you how she seemed to us then, and how I gradually began to understand the rich context of her life and how that context affected her attempts at academic writing. I had no special advantages—nothing except time, and interest, and a willingness to do the unconventional. I had never been to Mali, so all I knew about it was what she told me and how I imagined her life as an international development worker in this ancient African empire, now one of the poorest nations in the world.

Madelaine came to the U.S. on her own somehow, unenrolled in a degree program, hoping to qualify for admission to a master's program at the Center for International Education at the University of Massachusetts. Her English was halting then, and she was hesitant about using it at all, preferring to speak French with her American colleagues at the Center who had worked in West Africa. Her elegant bearing and calm, thoughtful countenance seemed to reflect her regal heritage— she was descended from an ancient royal family in Mali—but her quick adoption of jeans and a university sweatshirt revealed her practical, egalitarian attitude; I could easily imagine her in her job back home, jouncing over potholes in an aid agency jeep in 120-degree heat, working without supplies, even basic ones like paper or pencils or blackboards, to train village women with little schooling themselves to promote adult literacy.

But transplanted into the context of the U.S. university classroom, Madelaine was reticent and seemed preoccupied during class discussions. Her professors wondered, at times, if she were totally lost, though when they asked for her comments, she would gamely grope for words to illustrate the point under discussion with an example from her experience in Mali. This disturbed one of her instructors a little; it is a pattern he sees, sometimes, in students from developing countries as well as in some U.S. involuntary minority students. "They rehash the same ideas," he told me. "It's almost as if they write the same paper over and over for every class—not literally, of course, but they seem stuck in their own situation, unable to generalize, unable to branch out and broaden themselves. After all, the purpose of graduate school is to see how practice can be informed by theory, to begin to think broadly about trends and percentages. With some of these students," he sighed, "you consider yourself lucky if you can get them to the technician level—you feel like even *that* is a significant accomplishment. But if they want to go on and become professionals they can't keep doing things just on the basis of what feels good and past experience. They've got to be able to stand back and say, 'This is a category of problems.' They have to be able to synthesize and see patterns, to move outside of their own experience—that's what a university education is all about."

What was even more disturbing than Madelaine's trouble in contributing to theoretical discussions, her instructors said, was that she didn't seem to be making much progress on her written work, although her evident popularity with U.S. students and her boisterous laugh in the hallways gave her instructors the feeling there was something interesting and important about her that they did not completely understand. Should they recommend her for admission to a formal program, they wondered? How much was she really getting out of her courses? Was English too much of a barrier? She had taken several intensive language courses already; would continuing these help her performance in class and get her started writing? Or was Madelaine unable, at this point, to grasp the content of the education courses, unprepared to think and analyze in complex ways—unprepared, in other words, to meet the standards of a good graduate school at a U.S. university?

My own contact with Madelaine began when I asked her if she was interested in doing a French-English language exchange with me, as I was hoping to be sent to Mali to do a teacher-training workshop and I needed to revive my dormant French language skills. We started by meeting two hours a week, one for her English and one for my French, but the sessions became so engrossing that they lasted longer and longer until finally we could not expect to meet for less than four hours at a time. We would stretch out on bamboo mats on the floor in Madelaine's student apartment, drinking beer or sipping Malian tea, talking about social and political development in Mali in one language or the other and looking over the papers she was trying to write for her courses.

I soon discovered, both through our discussions and from other graduate students who had worked with her in her own country, that

Madelaine is a leading feminist in Mali, one of the few outspoken women with social and political influence. In fact, her bold manner, her predilection for sharp commentary and her dedication to Malian women had gained her a certain notoriety with her colleagues at home. Once, she told me, a high-ranking official from a U.S. aid agency had come to Mali to propose a new program for women that would give them access to credit to start small businesses. As the only woman present at the meeting, Madelaine was invited to comment on his proposal, but instead of expressing the expected gratitude and enthusiastic agreement with whatever the foreign donors suggested, she said what was on her mind. "How can we be speaking of giving women credit," she asked, "when our government thinks so little of the rights of women that it doesn't even allow us to have social security numbers?" The U.S. official was embarrassed at this unexpected remark and her Malian co-workers were horrified, knowing such honesty could get her arrested and their agency disbanded. Though Madelaine was threatened with the loss of her job over this incident, she was not at all discouraged, she told me; in fact, it made her even more convinced that her country would never become a true democracy without the equal rights and participation of women.

It is in this context that Madelaine has started writing a twenty-page term paper for her class in "Gender Issues in International Development." The draft that she shows me starts with an outline that she has made in French, which in itself is about twenty-four pages long. This outline contains a chart covering two pages in her small, ornate handwriting that attempts to trace the condition of women through Malian history, from the roots of traditional society through the colonial era to the socialist government and up to the current military dictatorship, which is about to give way to a multiparty system through popular protest.[1]

As Madelaine works on this chart, which she has been doing for the last several weeks, she is excited by her own analysis—the way facts and trends and ideas seem to fit together to create a particular way of viewing the condition of women and the reasons for their oppression. As she thinks about her country's history, she tells me, she is becoming aware that women actually had more power in traditional society than they do now, for as the progression of governments created more and more repressive conditions, women lost more of their traditional rights, privileges, and societal esteem. And as women's power diminished, even the words used to refer to women and the proverbs applied to them became more aggressive. It is now said, for example, that the more a women suffers from her husband's abuse, the more her children will be blessed.

Madelaine has been trying to simplify her chart so that a few words or phrases will capture the complex ideas she has been discovering, for she wants to be able to share her analysis with the village women she works with. She tells me that she recently received a fax from a French priest in Mali, asking her to design a series of workshops on "Democracy, Women and the Church" for about fifty women from his parish. Madelaine and I spend one of our sessions brainstorming ways to get across the concept of democracy to unschooled, illiterate women— many of whom were married at age twelve or thirteen—and to encourage them to begin to do what was formerly unthinkable: evaluate and question their condition in the family, in the political process, even in the church itself. At the same time, she is working out another idea that has recently occurred to her: creating a network of village day care centers that could free women from some of their daily drudgery in order to be able to attend such workshops, to become literate, to have, as Madelaine says, "a period of reflection" away from the incessant demands of family, of day-to-day survival, just as she is using her time in the U.S. to reflect on the future of Malian women.

All these thoughts are filling Madelaine's head as she works on this paper, contributing to a pretty severe case of insomnia that has gone on now for some weeks. We have heard only recently of the success of the coup against the military dictatorship that controlled Mali's government, and Madelaine has been on the phone to her family every night, both to assure herself of their safety and to participate— if only from a distance—in the historical moment. She sees this as an ideal time to advocate for women's rights, and she is trying to figure out how to introduce discussion of the formalization of these rights at the national level. At the same time, she is aware that she is behind in her course work at the university and that it doesn't seem likely that she will catch up with it soon, given all the things that now occupy her mind. We joke that she is raising procrastination to new heights by working out a new constitution for Mali instead of writing her term papers.

But what do Madelaine's professors know of the things that occupy her mind these days? They know something about the political situation in Mali, even though it hasn't merited much attention in the news-papers, for Madelaine has spoken about it in class. They know of her background as a trainer for literacy workers and of her personal interest in feminism; these basic facts about Madelaine are hard to overlook. But when they ask her about her papers, she tells them that she will have them finished shortly and that English is a problem for her. This explanation is easy to give and easy to understand, and of course it is true. But because her instructors are not aware of the complexity of the context, it is hard for them to imagine the added difficulties that lie behind what they conceive of as a "language problem."

One of the thorniest of these difficulties is clarifying her idea of the audience for this paper. It would seem logical that she should be writing it with the tone, the vocabulary, the style and organization that are suitable for her professor and, by extension, the U.S. university, but Madelaine is not really thinking about them as she writes. Even while she is using a scholarly vocabulary to describe the complex situation, she is constantly asking herself how to represent this or that idea in pictures or graphs in order to get them across to the village women she works with. But how is she to combine these simple, pictorial representations with the concepts she is trying to work out for the university? She shows me a rough sketch of a graph that she has been trying to make that would show, in a simple and dramatic way, the loss of power that women suffered in the home and in society at the same time men's power plummeted under the military dictatorship. She has historical periods written on the horizontal axis, with the different regimes marked below them. On the vertical axis she has an arrow, with *"plus de pouvoir"* scribbled at the top and *"moins de pouvoir"* at the bottom. What she's trying to do now, she says, is to have this graph somehow also suggest the possibility of change in the future: if in the new multiparty system men will be able to regain their former power and even increase their rights, why couldn't women do the same?

For an academic audience, we agree, the horizontal axis should have some measurable index of power—"because if not," says Madelaine, "what are you plotting? The question is," she continues, "how do you measure power?" On paper, both men and women have had the vote for some time, she tells me, but this "power" is meaningless when the only choice has been either a "yes" for the dictator or a "no" for the dictator—no other candidates allowed. "Besides," she tells me, "there aren't any 'no' slips, only 'yes' ones." And as for other indications of lack of power, it's hard to measure the effect of degrading proverbs or epithets, and there is no reporting of domestic violence except by word of mouth.

So the conflict between different audience demands is holding up her progress on the paper; at the same time that she tries to work out some quantitative indicators for the university, she is also thinking that such measurements are unimportant for the rural audience who should, perhaps, be the real beneficiaries of her ideas. As for her primary audience, her instructor, Madelaine tells me she hardly knows her; she has never talked with her after class and so she has not thought about the extent to which she would have to explain the Malian reality in her paper. Telling me about her ideas had helped some, she says, as she now understands my confusion when she translates a proverb from Bambara, her maternal language, without enough explanation of the context or explicit statement of the relationship between the proverb and the point she is trying to make with it. But how well does she understand the western university audience, and how relevant is that understanding, really, in Madelaine's situation? We are fond of saying that knowledge is a social construct, created by communities to serve social and political purposes. But what is a student to do when two vastly different communities are vying for her attention?

Even if she weren't trying to bridge the gulf between the Malian and U.S. audiences for this paper, Madelaine would still have to negotiate three languages, cultures, and systems of thought. First, there is the matter of English. It seems clear from the way she reads aloud to me from journal articles for pronunciation practice that some of the vocabulary and cultural references are obscure to her, though she says she is keeping up with the reading. But while she is hesitant about her English, her functioning in it, I am discovering, is not particularly low, compared with that of other second-language graduate students. During our sessions together, when she forces herself to speak in English, her words come faster and more fluently the more she gets involved in explaining her ideas—the reverse of what seems to be happening to my French. Though she failed the TOEFL a few months back, she came in only three points below the score the university requires for graduate admissions. Thinking back over the questions she knew she missed, she remembered being confused by the term "thousand island," which she had been asked to define. She was incredulous when I told her it was a type of salad dressing, and when I showed her a bottle of it in the supermarket and explained that the "islands" are the little bits of pickle floating in the sauce, she laughed until she cried.

So although Madelaine can function in English just as well as many other international students, she still lacks confidence and therefore chooses to write—at the idea stage, at least—in French, the language of her undergraduate education in Mali. But although French is the language of her academic and professional life back home, it is also the language of a people for whom Madelaine has little respect. She is put off by the "snobbism" of the French, she tells me, and especially by their overt claim that Malian culture is "uncivilized" compared with their own "superior" civilization. But at the same time that Madelaine is angrily resisting this epithet and the colonialist assumptions that go with it, she is bold enough to confront whatever truth there might be in this point of view. During a panel discussion at a recent conference, she tells me, she challenged a Malian colleague on his insistence that the west learn from developing nations as well as the other way around. "What does the west really have to learn from us?" she demanded. "Tell me, what is the curriculum?"

Madelaine is acutely aware of her emotions about this issue and, indeed, has chosen to get her degree at an English-speaking institution rather than go to France, where she would at least be fluent. "I couldn't face that smug, superior attitude every day. I would rather struggle with English," she says, choosing to forget, for the moment, the U.S. undergraduate who had passed us in a car the day before and, catching sight of Madelaine's ebony skin and shoulder-length tresses, had made an enormously loud and obscene retching noise in our direction.

Language, culture, colonialism, racism, all are intertwined in the depths of Madelaine's "language problem." And if this were not complex enough, when she thinks in Bambara, which she begins to do when she thinks of her rural audience, she begins to see things concretely and holistically, to put things in terms of narratives and descriptions that provide the context for the listener's analysis instead of thinking in abstractions, with the clear and direct interconnections between ideas that would make her own interpretation more accessible to her western audience. In addition, her personal communicative style—despite the Malian tendency for indirection and the French predilection for delicacy and detail—is earthy and direct; she is used to saying what is on her mind.

In addition to problems of audience and the complexities inherent in the languages and cultures that influence her thinking, Madelaine is falling into other difficulties faced by many world majority students— the problems of referencing, the tendency to indirection and overgeneralization, the reluctance to give a personal opinion in an academic paper. But here, too, new complications crop up. I had suggested that she use written sources to document the historical data she is using, but she reminds me that nothing much is written down in Mali; whoever has written a history is probably French and is almost certainly male, and she does not really trust these perspectives, at least for the purpose of this paper. History is traditionally passed down orally, through the *griots,* but nowadays, Madelaine says, the *griots* are nothing more than a mouthpiece for the dictator and are employed to sing the praises of the powerful, rather than teaching the history of times past. Madelaine is disgusted with this situation and is critical of the tapes of "authentic" *griot* music brought back from Mali by her American roommate, who does not speak Bambara fluently enough to catch the sycophantic purpose behind them.[2]

Madelaine's tendency to write rather vaguely, without defining terms, also seems to follow the typical pattern of students from cultures that value indirection, but when I suggest that she explain a little more about the meaning of words like "democracy" in the Malian context, Madelaine shakes her head. "No," she says, " 'democracy' hasn't been defined yet; it is barely born." If she stopped to try to define words like "power" and "domination" and "freedom" and "democracy," she tells me with a laugh, her insomnia might become terminal.

All these difficulties spill over into her second overdue paper, one on participatory evaluation, the latest trend in foreign development assistance. The idea is that the people who are the beneficiaries of grass-roots development projects—new literates, for example—should participate in the evaluation of their program. It is not enough any more to send a consultant from Washington to measure the reading ability of the literacy classes after the lessons are over, or to count the number of dropouts, or even to interview participants and ask them how they like the program. Now the idea is that the people themselves should have the opportunity to decide how they would measure success, design the evaluation instruments, and carry out the evaluation itself. This method puts more power into the hands of the poor, thus increasing their investment in the projects and their willingness to make changes in their lives.

Madelaine is sitting at the computer, thinking about the paper that she has to write giving her "viewpoint" about participatory evaluation. She stares at the blank screen for a long time. "What is a viewpoint?" she asks me finally. "Does that mean my personal opinion about these issues?"

"That's right."

"I think we're still stuck in the third world method of writing papers," she says. "I'm afraid to give my point of view because I am writing to a teacher, and the teacher knows everything, the teacher is the authority." She swivels her chair around to look at me, and we both start to laugh, thinking of the professor for this class, so mild, so supportive of difference of opinion, so removed from the context of her culture.

But knowing Madelaine, I am not surprised to discover that she does have a viewpoint on the subject, even though she doesn't find it appropriate to state it in her paper. "I don't believe in participatory evaluation," she says. "How can a technique that comes from any outside funder be 'participatory'? This inherently sets up a power relationship. The donor has the money and wants to stay in the business of giving it. The outside consultant wants to keep on getting jobs evaluating programs or, with this new approach, teaching people how to evaluate their own projects. The Malian aid agencies—the NGOs[3]—which spend the money and set up the programs, want to continue to stay in business. The people want the projects to continue if only because they bring a few new activities and materials into their impoverished environment. Everyone has their vested interests," she continues, her voice rising. "And everyone bullshits each other to show their project in the best possible light—the people, the NGOs, the outside consultant, the U.S. aid agency. So participatory evaluation is impossible. I think we should call it something else, like some kind of education," she says, "to get away from the idea, imposed by our dependency status, that our projects must be evaluated at all."

But how can she say this in her paper, she asks me. If she gives away the NGOs' "secret"—that they manufacture results for evaluations—the NGOs will suffer; they need the donor's money to support themselves. But if she doesn't say what she thinks, not only will she be unable to write the paper, but her anger at the whole international development scene, in which she is a key player, will continue to weigh her down. So what will be the use of staying in development work at all, she wonders. Why doesn't she just join the Malian women's caucus, which does nothing but pander to the government, or take a job in an air-conditioned office instead of driving over unpaved roads to remote villages out of some kind of vision of emancipating her countrywomen?

Madelaine agrees that writing what she really feels about this issue of participatory evaluation will help her think through her personal dilemma; she needs the period of reflection at a foreign university not so much for the degree, she tells me, although that will be a useful addition to her status and influence at home, but more to be able to have the time to think, to put her past experiences into perspective, to analyze current problems, to make charts and tear them up and make other ones, to draft a hypothetical constitution ("if women are allowed rights under the new regime, which is unlikely," she says wryly), to plan workshops, to do presentations at conferences and network with colleagues around the U.S., to make linkages between

U.S. universities and women's programs in Mali. And all this has a tendency to overshadow the university's expectation that she think and write and contribute to class discussion in particular ways. The university doesn't expect nearly as much of its students as Madelaine seems compelled by an inner fire to give.

Remember that to her professors—who haven't had the privilege of listening to her long enough and in congenial enough surroundings to hear what she has to tell us—Madelaine looks like a student with a language problem who has a tendency to dwell upon her own past experience and relate everything she learns to that experience, and whose papers—if she does manage to hand them in—are bound to contain some puzzling gaps in logic and continuity, inadequate referencing, some strange-looking visuals that look like a combination of a graph and a billboard, and a lot of shallow generalities that do not seem to even hint at any particular point of view.

But even after the story behind these surface features comes clear, even after we can say more confidently *why* these features are there, we still may have to ask ourselves if we are ready to provide the support and the personal attention Madelaine needs to bridge her multiple worlds. Her triple language-culture negotiation will take time to work through, time which instructors don't often have. She may need a good deal of convincing to overcome her difficulty in expressing her very strong, very analytical viewpoints in her papers. Her obsession with the Malian context will not likely flag, nor should it, given the necessity for energetic, original thinking on the problems that aid agencies, with all their western funding and foreign consultants, have not been able to solve. And her audience problem will not go away as long as Madelaine puts Malian women before her U.S. university professors.

And at the same time, we might also wonder if the university is prepared to open itself to Madelaine's way of seeing the world. Are we ready to imagine knowledge differently? Are we willing to spend time learning the details of vastly different cultural contexts? Are we persistent enough to listen to the gaps and silences until we hear, in the distance, the voices of thousand-year-old intellectual traditions? Madelaine might say that she doesn't expect all this of us. It would be enough if we would understand her struggles with English and give her a little more time to finish her papers. But if we believe we are ready for such a profound rethinking of the goals and purposes of the university, if we are ready to listen to the world, "higher education" will never be the same.

Notes

Chapter 1. Frustrations

1. In the excerpts that follow, and throughout this book, I have corrected the grammar in the writing and verbal comments of second-language students so that the reader can focus on the meaning of what they have to say. All students' names have been changed, though I have tried to match names with cultures, personalities, and in some cases with degree of "westernization." Thus a student whose real name is Grace Chen might be renamed Anita Wong rather than Su-ping Wong.

Chapter 2. Worldwide Strategies for Indirection

1. Anthropologist Richard A. Schweder notes in *Thinking through Cultures* (1991) that rich, contextual detail in personal and social description has been found by observers in Africa, Central America, the South Pacific, and Central Asia. The "context-dependent person," or "holist," is "convinced that objects and events are necessarily altered by the relations into which they enter [and thus] is theoretically primed to contextualize objects and events, and theoretically disinclined to appraise things *in vacuo*, in the abstract" (153).

For a discussion of digression in Hindi expository prose, see Kachru (1982), "Linguistics and Written Discourse in Particular Languages: Contrastive Studies: English and Hindi."

2. An important exception is African American communicative style, which is more direct, more "confrontational" even than white, mainstream U.S. culture. See Chapter 6 in this book and Kochman (1981), *Black and White Styles in Conflict.*

3. See, for example, Day (1992), *Scientific English: A Guide for Scientists and Other Professionals;* Bazerman (1988), *Shaping Written Knowledge: The Genre and Activity of the Experimental Article in Science;* Maimon (1983), "Maps and Genres: Exploring Connections in the Arts and Sciences"; MacDonald (1987), "Problem Definition in Academic Writing"; Elbow (1991), "Reflections on Academic Discourse"; and McGann (1992), *Critical Thinking and Writing in the Disciplines.*

4. For an interesting discussion of how young children learn discourse strategies in Athabaskan culture, see Scollon and Scollon (1981), *Narrative, Literacy, and Face in Interethnic Communication.*

5. Whorf (1956), *Language, Thought and Reality.*

6. See, for example, Yang (1986), "Chinese Personality and Its Change."

7. See Ong (1982), *Orality and Literacy;* Goody (1986), *The Logic of Writing and the Organization of Society;* and Havelock (1963), *Preface to Plato.*

8. For another example of indirect, digressive writing from a Latin cultural context, see Paulo Freire's *Pedagogy of the Oppressed* (1986).

9. Of course within the continents of Asia, Africa, and Latin America there are hundreds of linguistic and cultural groups; African cultures, for example, are at least as different from each other as, say, Finland is from Italy in language, outlook, national "character," and communication style. But when we look broadly across groups that inhabit particular areas of the world or that are strongly linked by their history, it is possible to see important similarities as well. And although I risk oversimplification by speaking of "Asian culture" or the "Euro-American mainstream," or by contrasting "world majority cultures" to "western culture," I do this to draw attention to broad similarities within a world of enormous diversity.

10. J. O. Yum's article, "The Impact of Confucianism on Interpersonal Relationships and Communication Patterns in East Asia" (1991), contains a good general discussion of indirect communication strategies and contrasts receiver-centered and sender-centered communication.

11. See also Dunlap (1990), "Language and Power: Teaching Writing to Third World Graduate Students in U.S. Planning Schools."

12. For an interesting discussion of "coherence," the guidelines within which speakers and writers of various languages are expected to stay, see Johns (1986), "Coherence and Academic Writing: Some Definitions and Suggestions for Teaching"; and Carrell (1984), "The Effects of Rhetorical Organization on ESL Readers."

Chapter 3. "In Solidarity": The Voice of the Collectivity

1. Werner and Bower (1982), *Helping Health Workers Learn,* 9–22.

2. See, for example, Linteau, Durucher, and Robert (1983), *Quebec: A History 1867–1929;* Mathieu and Lacoursière (1991), *Les mémoires Québecoises;* and Young and Dickinson (1988), *A Short History of Quebec: A Socioeconomic Perspective.*

3. A study by a cross-cultural communication specialist, Geert Hofstede, of the values of employees working in subsidiaries of IBM, ranks fifty countries on a continuum between individualism and collectivism. At the individualism end, the U.S. ranks first, followed by Australia, Great Britain, and other western countries. India ranks highest of the nonwestern countries on individualism, followed immediately by Japan. Starting from the collectivism end of the scale, Guatemala holds first place, followed by Panama, Venezuela, Colombia, Indonesia, Pakistan, Costa Rica, Peru, Taiwan, and South Korea, in that order (Hofstede 1991, 53).

Though in general, western countries are the most individualistic, several cultures outside the western tradition not studied by Hofstede place even more emphasis on the individual. In Athabaskan culture, studied by Scollon and Scollon (1981), "Athabaskans offer and expect in return a high degree of respect for a person's individuality, his right to be independent, autonomous, and different from others" (7). This individuality, even more pronounced than that of mainstream Americans, is part of the Athabaskan "bush consciousness" that requires the individual to be "a viable unit of survival under extremes of isolation and environmental duress." While the average Athabaskan never has to "feed, house, and clothe himself for months with nothing but what he can carry himself in deep snow at perhaps −40 degrees" (103), all individuals are taught to be mentally prepared to do so from the time they are small children. The Scollons point out how such environmental contingencies have created a culturally specific world view and communicative style that affect the acquisition of literacy and both oral and written discourse patterns. For other studies of individualism-collectivism see, for example, Triandis et al. (1988), "Individualism and Collectivism: Cross-Cultural Perspectives on Self-Ingroup Relationships."

4. See Triandis, Brislin, and Hui (1988), "Cross-Cultural Training across the Individualism-Collectivism Divide." The "new discovery" by western social constructionists that knowledge is created by communities and that it is powerful and unifying to study and write and dialogue together can perhaps be compared with the "new discovery" by people in collectivist societies like Japan that knowledge is created by individuals and that it can feel powerful and liberating to find one's own voice. Neither culture is conceptualizing the idea in quite the same terms as the other, and both are struggling against conservative forces that would preserve their culture's world view.

5. An example of the rhetoric of group cohesion in an individualist context is a U.S. political convention, where both oral and written words are designed to generate enthusiasm for a body of ideas and to gloss over factional and individual differences. Of course, individuals retain their own opinions in this context, just as in collectivist societies the need for an appearance of unity precludes personal differences but does not obliterate them.

6. For a good example of a writer's effective use of a controlled academic tone with emotionally charged subject matter, see Ogbu (1988), "Literacy and Schooling in Subordinate Cultures: The Case of Black Americans."

7. "Harper's Forum: What Is Ours to Defend?" (La Roque 1988).

Chapter 4. "What Is Ancient Is Also Original"

1. The total number of Chinese characters is much greater, about 43,000.

2. I have noticed these tendencies in training teachers in Côte d'Ivoire and India and in visiting schools and talking with teachers in those countries as well as in Togo and the Solomon Islands. Graduate students from Japan, China, Chile, Colombia, Nepal, India, and many other world majority cultures offered me similar observations from their own experience.

3. The term and the idea come from the observations of the American and Japanese co-authors Nancy Sakamoto and Reiko Naotsuka (1982), *Polite Fictions*.

4. See Hofstede (1991), *Cultures and Organizations: Software of the Mind*. In cultures with a high power-distance index, IBM managers prefer an autocratic or a paternalistic style rather than a consultative style in their relations with both their subordinates and their superiors. Countries that rate high on power distance correspond to a certain extent with collectivist cultures: Latin American, African, and Asian countries tend to lie at the high end of the scale, while northern European countries cluster at the lower end. The

U.S. is near the low end, but higher in power distance than the Scandinavian countries, Canada, Australia, and New Zealand.

Chapter 5. Something Inside Is Saying No

1. In fact, in Nepal, a teacher might not make this criticism because there, as Surya is telling us, the writing is *expected* to be indirect. But he uses this as an example to do exactly what he is illustrating: talking about another person in order to tell me gently how I and other instructors might have talked to him about style change without hurting his feelings.

2. A handout in my writing class: Shen (1989), "The Classroom and the Wider Culture: Identity as a Key to Learning English Composition."

3. For more of the Chilean context, see, for example, Latin America Bureau (1983), *Chile, the Pinochet Decade: The Rise and Fall of the Chicago Boys.*

4. Readers interested in a detailed understanding of how cultural and social meanings affect words, sentences, and paragraphs in specific languages might start by referring to the 1982 *Annual Review of Applied Linguistics.* To give an idea of the interesting complexity involved, William Leap mentions that in the Ute language of Native Americans in northeast Utah there are at least eight ways to order the grammatical and lexical items in the sentence "The boy is eating an apple," depending on such things as the band affiliation of the speaker, residence, facility in the Ute language, and other factors. Thus Ute speakers "complain that written Ute, even when written in a writing system developed by native speakers, deprives the language of its flexibility" (Leap 1982, 26).

5. The peer tutors who work in Michigan's Writing Program are juniors and seniors who have been trained by the department in a series of courses that combine theory, educational methods (including a little on second-language teaching and cultural communicative styles), and practical tutoring experience. The peer tutors are popular among students and are consistently rated high on student evaluations.

Chapter 6. Stigma and Resistance

1. See Ogbu (1991a, 5), "Cultural Models and Educational Strategies of Non-dominant Peoples." Ogbu is considered by many to be one of the world's leading educational anthropologists. He came to the U.S. from Nigeria to study for his bachelor's, master's, and doctoral degrees at the University of California, Berkeley, where he continues to teach and do research.

2. See Lee (1991), "Koreans in Japan and the United States." Youngsook Lee studies Asian achievement patterns at the Korean Educational Development Institute.

3. At the end of the war, with the liberation of Korea from Japanese colonialism, about a million and a half Koreans returned home, but more than 600,000 were obliged to stay on because of Allied orders forbidding repatriates from taking any more than a paltry sum of money out of the country. Thus they remained, "a segregated, poor and persecuted minority in

the midst of an increasingly affluent Japan" (Goldstein 1972, quoted in Y. Lee 1991, 142).

4. K. Lee 1983, in Y. Lee 1991, 155.

5. These and other prohibitions apply to the more than 670,000 Koreans in Japan today who have not become citizens. Koreans are reluctant to apply for citizenship for a number of reasons, including ineligibility because of minor legal infractions and the psychological effects of identifying themselves with people who hold them in contempt (Y. Lee 1991).

6. Fully half of the students in special education classes in neighborhoods that Shimahara (1991) studied were Burakumin, though they made up only 30 percent of the elementary school population and 5 percent of the middle school students.

7. Shimahara (1991, 346). In fact, "assimilation education" programs were so intensive that funds spent per child on minority children were three times those spent on mainstream Japanese children.

8. Other ethnic groups whose academic performance has been studied in two locations are the Finns in Sweden (where they are involuntary minorities—"more or less like ex-colonials," says Ogbu—because Sweden ruled Finland for centuries) compared with the Finns in Australia, where they do well as voluntary immigrants; West Indians in Britain, where they are doing poorly, and in the U.S. and Canada, where they do better than African Americans; Polynesians, who do well as immigrants to New Zealand, as compared with the native Maoris, who are similar to Polynesians in language and culture but were incorporated involuntarily into New Zealand society in much the same way Native Americans were in the U.S. (Ogbu 1991a, 5).

9. This similarity between the denial of male privilege by men and the denial of white privilege by whites has been discussed by others; see, for example, McIntosh (1989), "White Privilege: Unpacking the Invisible Knapsack."

10. An extreme example of nonrecognition: A Pennsylvania first-grade teacher asked the only two black students in her classroom to get up on a table and pretend they were slaves being sold at an auction. "I did not view it as racial," the teacher said, after the children's parents protested. "I wanted to teach the children about prejudice" (*New York Times* 1993, A7N).

11. Claude Steele is the twin brother of Shelby Steele, author of the controversial bestseller *The Content of Our Character* (1990), which argues that racism is no longer a major barrier for blacks in U.S. society. The different approaches taken by these brothers symbolize, perhaps, the vigorous and healthy diversity of opinion within the black community about the nature of the problem and its possible solutions.

12. The feelings and behavior Campbell describes are strikingly similar to those of Burakumin students in Japan. Shimahara reports: "Majority students at both the schools I studied were keenly aware that Burakumin students were often aggressive, intimidating, temperamental, violent and vengeful. Yet, these same minority students, according to their teachers, were anxious, insecure, suspicious and apprehensive about majority children" (Shimahara 1991, 340).

13. The expression is Ogbu's (1991a, 13).

14. See Smitherman (1986), *Talkin and Testifyin: The Language of Black America*. "Neighborhood style" is not typical of all African Americans, of course, even if they live in black neighborhoods. "It's a family thing," students say. Some families use mainstream dialect and communicative style exclusively, others use one or the other on different occasions, while still others incorporate some features of the dominant culture into their predominantly black cultural style or vice versa.

15. See, for example, Genovese (1974), *Roll, Jordan, Roll: The World the Slaves Made*; Smitherman (1986), *Talkin and Testifyin: The Language of Black America*; and Kochman (1981), *Black and White Styles in Conflict*.

16. Mphahlele (1993, 180), "Educating the Imagination." For more insight into African epistemology, see Asante (1987), *The Afrocentric Idea*.

17. For an analysis that places more significance on the differences between African American and mainstream culture, see Hale-Benson (1986), *Black Children: Their Roots, Cultures, and Learning Styles*.

18. For more on the changes that college students of both dominant and targeted groups go through in the development of their racial identity, see Hardiman and Jackson (1992), "Racial Identity Development: Understanding Racial Dynamics in College Classrooms and on Campus."

19. For more understanding of the origins, purposes, and grammar of Black English, see Jordan (1988), "Nobody Mean More to Me Than You and the Future Life of Willie Jordan." Because black culture has been threatened by annihilation, the language is structured to affirm that "we exist, that we are present" (367). Thus it "abhors all abstraction," uses no passive voice, insists on directness, brevity and clarity, and largely omits the verb "to be," substituting verbs of greater precision and emotional force.

Chapter 7. Helping World Majority Students Make Sense of University Expectations

1. Radical Brazilian educator Paulo Freire, whose literacy programs are a model for empowerment education worldwide, is surprisingly critical of the cultural aspects of his country's formal education system. What I see as legitimate cultural differences in communicative style and world view, Freire sees as a cultural "habit of submission" (1981, 23) to the intellectual and political elite fostered by the colonial plantation system and a history of slavery. "Our traditional curriculum, disconnected from life, centered on words emptied of the reality they are meant to represent, lacking in concrete activity, could never develop a critical consciousness. Indeed, its own naive dependence on high-sounding phrases, reliance on rote and tendency toward abstractness actually intensified our naivete" (37).

Epilogue

1. In 1992, Mali became one of the first African nations to achieve a peaceful transition to democracy.

2. With the advent of the multiparty system, Malian *griots* were faced with unemployment, for such praise-songs were no longer in demand. Seizing the moment, Madelaine organized a *"griot* workshop" where *griots* and street

theater performers met to consider the idea of creating new songs to spread the benefits of literacy, family planning, and women's rights to the rural population. This workshop, carried out almost entirely in song and facilitated by African American educators who were themselves singers, actors, and social change agents in the U.S., attracted triple the expected number of Malian participants.

3. In developing countries, Non-Governmental Organizations, or NGOs, operate alongside of government programs to improve health, education, and well-being of the grass-roots population. Their projects tend to be small and localized and are almost always dependent for funding on large international aid agencies such as the United States Agency for International Development (USAID) and the World Bank.

Works Cited

Altman, L. K. (1992, December 20). U.S. moves to replace Japanese head of W.H.O. *New York Times*, 1.

Asante, M. K. (1987). *The Afrocentric idea.* Philadelphia: Temple University Press.

Ashton-Warner, S. [1963] (1986). *Teacher* (17). New York: Simon and Schuster.

Bazerman, C. (1988). *Shaping written knowledge: The genre and activity of the experimental article in science.* Madison: University of Wisconsin Press.

Belenky, M. F., Clinchy, B. M., Goldberger, N. R., and Tarule, J. M. (1986). *Women's ways of knowing: The development of self, voice, and mind.* New York: Basic Books.

Bernal, M. (1987). *Black Athena: The Afroasiatic roots of classical civilization: Vol. I. The fabrication of ancient Greece, 1785–1985.* New Brunswick, NJ: Rutgers University Press.

Campbell, B. M. (1993, January 18). *Opening address, Martin Luther King Day.* Ann Arbor: Power Center, University of Michigan.

Carrell, P. (1984, September). The effects of rhetorical organization on ESL readers. *TESOL Quarterly, 18*(3), 441–469.

Day, R. A. (1992). *Scientific English: A guide for scientists and other professionals.* Phoenix, AZ: Oryx Press.

de Tocqueville, A. [1840] (1990). *Democracy in America* (Vol. II). New York: Random House, Vintage Books Edition.

Dunlap, L. (1990). Language and power: Teaching writing to third world graduate students in U.S. planning schools. In B. Sanyal (Ed.), *Breaking the boundaries: A one-world approach to planning education.* New York: Plenum Press.

Elbow, P. (1991, February). Reflections on academic discourse: How it relates to freshmen and colleagues. *College English, 53*(2), 135–155.

Evangelauf, J. (1993, January 20). Number of minority students in colleges rose by 9% from 1990 to 1991, U.S. reports. *Chronicle of Higher Education,* A30–31.

Fanon, F. (1967). *Black skin, white masks.* New York: Grove Press.

Freire, P. [1973] (1981). *Education as the practice of freedom.* New York: Continuum.

———. [1970] (1986). *Pedagogy of the oppressed.* New York: Continuum.

Gardner, H. (1989). *To open minds: Chinese clues to the dilemma of contemporary education.* New York: Pantheon Books.

Genovese, E. (1974). *Roll, Jordan, roll: The world the slaves made.* New York: Random House.

Goody, J. (1986). *The logic of writing and the organization of society.* London: Cambridge University Press.

Hale-Benson, J. E. (1986). *Black children: Their roots, culture, and learning styles.* Baltimore: Johns Hopkins University Press.

Hall, E. T. (1976). *Beyond culture.* Garden City, NY: Doubleday, Anchor Press.

Hardiman, R., and Jackson, B. (1992, Winter). Racial identity development: Understanding racial dynamics in college classrooms and on campus. *New Directions for Teaching and Learning, 52,* 21–37.

Havelock, E. A. (1963). *Preface to Plato.* Cambridge, MA: Harvard University Press.

Hofstede, G. (1991). *Cultures and organizations: Software of the mind.* New York: McGraw Hill.

Jain, N. C. (1988). World view and cultural patterns of India. In L. A. Samovar and R. E. Porter (Eds.), *Intercultural communication: A reader.* Belmont, CA: Wadsworth Publishing.

Johns, A. M. (1986, June). Coherence and academic writing: Some definitions and suggestions for teaching. *TESOL Quarterly, 20*(2), 247–265.

Jordan, J. (1988, August). Nobody mean more to me than you and the future life of Willie Jordan. *Harvard Educational Review, 58*(3), 363–374.

Kachru, Y. (1982). Linguistics and written discourse in particular languages: Contrastive studies: English and Hindi. In *Annual Review of Applied Linguistics,* 50–77. Rowley, MA: Newbury House.

Kaplan, R. B. (1966). Cultural thought patterns in inter-cultural education. *Language Learning, 16,* 1–20.

———. (1972). *The anatomy of rhetoric: Prolegomena to a functional theory of rhetoric.* Philadelphia: Center for Curriculum Development.

———. (1982). An introduction to the study of written texts: The "discourse compact." In *Annual Review of Applied Linguistics,* 138–151. Rowley, MA: Newbury House.

Kochman, T. (1981). *Black and white styles in conflict.* Chicago: University of Chicago Press.

Laney, C. (1993). The black father described. In D. Campbell, *Easy writer* (3rd ed.). New York: HarperCollins.

La Roque, G. R. (1988, July). Harper's Forum: What is ours to defend? A military strategy for the 1990s. *Harper's Magazine,* 39–50.

Latin America Bureau. (1983). *Chile, the Pinochet decade: The rise and fall of the Chicago Boys.* London: Author.

Leap, W. (1982). Linguistics and written discourse in particular languages: Contrastive studies: English and American Indian languages. In *Annual Review of Applied Linguistics,* 24–37. Rowley, MA: Newbury House.

Lee, Y. (1991). Koreans in Japan and the United States. In M. A. Gibson and J. Ogbu (Eds.), *Minority status and schooling: A comparative study of immigrant and involuntary minorities.* New York: Garland Publishing.

Linteau, P. A., Durucher, R., and Robert, J. C. (1983). *Quebec: A history 1867–1929* (Robert Chodos, Trans.). Toronto: James Lorimer.

Liu, I. M. (1986). Chinese cognition. In M. H. Bond (Ed.), *The psychology of the Chinese people*. New York: Oxford University Press.

MacDonald, S. P. (1987, March). Problem definition in academic writing. *College English, 49*(3), 315–331.

Magner, D. K. (1992, April 1). Professor takes aim at blacks' racial vulnerability. *Chronicle of Higher Education*, A5.

McGann, M. E. (1992). *Critical thinking and writing in the disciplines*. Boston: Allyn & Bacon.

McIntosh, P. (1989, July/August). White privilege: Unpacking the invisible knapsack. *Peace and Freedom*, 10–12.

Maimon, E. P. (1983). Maps and genres: Exploring connections in the arts and sciences. In W. Horner (Ed.), *Composition and literature: Bridging the gap*. Chicago: University of Chicago Press.

Mathieu, J., and Lacoursière, J. (1991). *Les mémoires Québecoises*. Sainte Foy, PQ: Les Presses de l'Université Laval.

Mead, M. (1970). *Culture and commitment: A study of the generation gap*. Garden City, NY: Natural History Press/Doubleday.

Mphahlele, E. (1993, February). Educating the imagination. *College English, 55*(2), 179–186.

Nakamura, S. (1992). Standing between where I come from and where I am living now. In *Prism: Diverse perspectives from a university community*. Ann Arbor: English Composition Board, University of Michigan.

New York Times. (1993, January 22). Mock slave lesson prompts an outcry by pupils' parents, A7N.

Ogbu, J. (1988). Literacy and schooling in subordinate cultures: The case of black Americans. In E. R. Kintgen, B. M. Kroll, and M. Rose (Eds.), *Perspectives on literacy*. Carbondale: Southern Illinois University Press.

———. (1991a). Cultural models and educational strategies of non-dominant peoples. *The 1989 Catherine Molony Memorial Lecture*. New York: The City College Workshop Center.

———. (1991b). Immigrant and involuntary minorities in comparative perspective. In M. A. Gibson and J. Ogbu (Eds.), *Minority status and schooling: A comparative study of immigrant and involuntary minorities*. New York: Garland Publishing.

———. (1991c). Low school performance as an adaptation: The case of blacks in Stockton, California. In M. A. Gibson and J. Ogbu (Eds.), *Minority status and schooling: A comparative study of immigrant and involuntary minorities*. New York: Garland Publishing.

Ong, W. (1982). *Orality and literacy: The technologizing of the word*. New York: Methuen.

Peace Corps Togo. (1988). Field documents.

Sakamoto, N., and Naotsuka, R. (1982). *Polite fictions*. Tokyo: Kinseido Press.

Schweder, R. A. (1991). *Thinking through cultures: Expeditions in cultural psychology*. Cambridge, MA: Harvard University Press.

Scollon, R., and Scollon, S. B. K. (1981). *Narrative, literacy, and face in interethnic communication.* Norwood, NJ: Ablex.

Shen, F. (1989, December). The classroom and the wider culture: Identity as a key to learning English composition. Staffroom Interchange. *College Composition and Communication, 40*(4), 459–466.

Shimahara, N. K. (1991). Social mobility and education: Burakumin in Japan. In M. A. Gibson and J. Ogbu (Eds.), *Minority status and schooling: A comparative study of immigrant and involuntary minorities.* New York: Garland Publishing.

Smitherman, G. (1986). *Talkin and testifyin: The language of Black America.* Detroit: Wayne State University Press.

Steele, C. (1992, April). Race and the schooling of black Americans. *The Atlantic, 269,* 68–72.

Steele, S. (1990). *The content of our character: A new vision of race in America.* New York: St. Martin Press.

Triandis, H. C., Bontempo, R., Villareal, M. J., Asai, M., and Lucca, N. (1988). Individualism and collectivism: Cross-cultural perspectives on self-ingroup relationships. *Journal of Personality and Social Psychology, 54*(2), 323–338.

Triandis, H. C., Brislin, R. W., and Hui, H. (1988). Cross-cultural training across the individualism-collectivism divide. In L. A. Samovar and R. E. Porter (Eds.), *Intercultural communication: A reader.* Belmont, CA: Wadsworth Publishing.

UNESCO. (1987). *Histoire générale de l'Afrique.* Paris: Présence Africaine.

Werner, D., and Bower, B. (1982). *Helping health workers learn: A book of methods, aids, and ideas for instructors at the village level.* Palo Alto, CA: Hesperian Foundation.

Whitten, L. (1992). Survival conflict and survival guilt in African-American college students. In M. Lang and C. A. Ford (Eds.), *Strategies for retaining minority students in higher education.* Springfield, IL: Charles Thomas.

Whorf, B. L. (1956). *Language, thought and reality.* Cambridge, MA: MIT Press.

Yang, K. S. (1986). Chinese personality and its change. In M. H. Bond (Ed.), *The psychology of the Chinese people.* New York: Oxford University Press.

Young, B. J., and Dickinson, J. A. (1988). *A short history of Quebec: A socio-economic perspective.* Toronto: Copp Clark Pitman.

Yum, J. O. (1991). The impact of Confucianism on interpersonal relationships and communication patterns in East Asia. In L. A. Samovar and R. E. Porter (Eds.), *Intercultural communication: A reader.* Belmont, CA: Wadsworth Publishing.

Resources for Research, Teaching, and Cross-Cultural Understanding

This list is intended only to help you get started; it is much too short to give a comprehensive overview of the many fields it encompasses. To pursue your own particular interests further, check the ERIC (Educational Resources Information Center) database, which contains synopses of written resources in the field of education.

History, Geography, Languages of Specific Countries and Cultures

Lonely Planet (updated yearly). Travel series for various countries and areas of the world, for example, Iran, West Africa. Berkeley, CA: Lonely Planet Publications.

Takaki, R. (1989). *Strangers from a different shore: A history of Asian Americans.* Boston: Little, Brown.

————. (1993). *A different mirror: A history of multicultural America.* Boston: Little, Brown.

U.S. State Department (various). Country studies for background briefing purposes. The series covers most countries (for example, *India: A country study*) and is available in university libraries. Washington, D.C.: U.S. State Department, Bureau of Public Affairs.

Cultural Differences

Althen, G. (1988). *American ways: A guide for foreigners.* Yarmouth, ME: Intercultural Press.

Asante, M. K., and Gudykunst, W. B. (Eds.). (1989). *Handbook of international and intercultural communication.* Newbury Park, CA: Sage Publications.

Barnlund, D. C. (1975). *Public and private self in Japan and the United States.* Yarmouth, ME: Intercultural Press.

Bond, M. H. (Ed.). (1986). *The psychology of the Chinese people.* New York: Oxford University Press.

Condon, J. C. (1984). *With respect to the Japanese: A guide for Americans.* Yarmouth, ME: Intercultural Press.

————. (1985). *Good neighbors: Communicating with Mexicans.* Yarmouth, ME: Intercultural Press.

Fieg, J. P. (1989). *A common core: Thais and Americans.* Yarmouth, ME: Intercultural Press.

Hall, E. T. (1959). *The silent language.* Garden City, NY: Anchor Press.

————. (1976). *Beyond culture.* Garden City, NY: Doubleday, Anchor Press.

Hall, M. R. (1989). *Understanding cultural differences: Keys to success in West Germany, France and the United States.* Yarmouth, ME: Intercultural Press.

Hecht, M. L., Collier, M. J., and Ribeau, S. A. (1993). *African American communication: Ethnic identity and cultural interpretation.* Newbury Park, CA: Sage Publications.

Hofstede, G. (1984). *Culture's consequences: International differences in work-related values.* Newbury Park, CA: Sage Publications.

———. (1991). *Cultures and organizations: Software of the mind.* New York: McGraw Hill.

Jain, N. C. (1988). World view and cultural patterns of India. In L. A. Samovar and R. E. Porter (Eds.), *Intercultural communication: A reader.* Belmont, CA: Wadsworth Publishing.

Kochman, T. (1981). *Black and white styles in conflict.* Chicago: University of Chicago Press.

Locust, C. (1988, August). Wounding the spirit: Discrimination and traditional American Indian belief systems. *Harvard Educational Review, 58*(3), 315–330.

Markus, H. R., and Kitayama, S. (1991, April). Culture and the self: Implications for cognition, emotion, and motivation. *Psychological Review, 98*(2), 224–253.

Nydell, M. K. (1987). *Understanding Arabs: A guide for westerners.* Yarmouth, ME: Intercultural Press.

Sakamoto, N., and Naotsuka, R. (1982). *Polite fictions.* Tokyo: Kinseido Press.

Scollon, R., and Scollon, S. B. K. (1981). *Narrative, literacy, and face in interethnic communication.* Norwood, NJ: Ablex.

Ting-Toomey, S., and Korzenny, F. (Eds.). (1991). *Cross-cultural interpersonal communication.* Newbury Park, CA: Sage Publications.

Wenzhong, H., and Grove, C. L. (1991). *Encountering the Chinese: A guide for Americans.* Yarmouth, ME: Intercultural Press.

Yum, J. O. (1991). The impact of Confucianism on interpersonal relationships and communication patterns in East Asia. In L. A. Samovar and R. E. Porter (Eds.), *Intercultural communication: A reader.* Belmont, CA: Wadsworth Publishing.

Individualism-Collectivism

Pratt, D. D. (1991). Conceptions of self within China and the United States: Contrasting foundations for adult education. *International Journal of Intercultural Relations, 15*(3), 285–310.

Triandis, H. (1986). Collectivism vs. individualism: A reconceptualization of a basic concept in cross-cultural psychology. In G. K. Verma and C. Bagley (Eds.), *Personality, cognition, and values: Cross-cultural perspectives on childhood and adolescence.* London: Macmillan.

———. (1989). The self and social behavior in differing cultural contexts. *Psychological Review, 96,* 506–520.

Triandis, H. C., Bontempo, R., Villareal, M. J., Asai, M., and Lucca, N. (1988). Individualism and collectivism: Cross-cultural perspectives on self-ingroup relationships. *Journal of Personality and Social Psychology, 54*(2), 323–338.

Tu, W. (1985). Selfhood and otherness in Confucian thought. In A. J. Marsella, G. DeVos, and F. L. K. Hsu (Eds.), *Culture and self: Asian and Western perspectives.* New York: Tavistock.

Wheeler, L., Reis, H., and Bond, M. (1989). Collectivism-individualism in everyday social life: The Middle Kingdom and the melting pot. *Journal of Personality and Social Psychology, 57,* 79–86.

Effects of Language on Writing

Carson, J. G. (1992). Becoming biliterate: First language influences. *Journal of Second Language Writing, 1*(1), 37–60.

Chang, S. J. (1982). Linguistics and written discourse in particular languages: Contrastive studies: English and Korean. In *Annual Review of Applied Linguistics,* 85–98. Rowley, MA: Newbury House.

Connor, U., and Kaplan, R. B. (Eds.). (1987). *Writing across languages: Analysis of L2 text.* Reading, MA: Addison-Wesley.

Hinds, J. (1982). Linguistics and written discourse in English and Japanese: A contrastive study (1978–1982). In *Annual Review of Applied Linguistics,* 78–84. Rowley, MA: Newbury House.

———. (1987). Reader versus writer responsibility: A new typology. In U. Connor and R. B. Kaplan (Eds.), *Writing across languages: Analysis of L2 text.* Reading, MA: Addison-Wesley.

Houghton, D., and Hoey, M. (1982). Linguistics and written discourse: Contrastive rhetorics. In *Annual Review of Applied Linguistics,* 2–22. Rowley, MA: Newbury House.

Kachru, Y. (1982). Linguistics and written discourse in particular languages: Contrastive studies: English and Hindi. In *Annual Review of Applied Linguistics,* 50–77. Rowley, MA: Newbury House.

———. (1988). Cognitive and cultural styles in second language acquisition. In *Annual Review of Applied Linguistics,* 149–163. Rowley, MA: Newbury House.

Kaplan, R. B. (1966). Cultural thought patterns in inter-cultural education. *Language Learning, 16,* 1–20.

———. (1972). *The anatomy of rhetoric: Prolegomena to a functional theory of rhetoric.* Philadelphia: Center for Curriculum Development.

———. (1982). An introduction to the study of written texts: The "discourse compact." In *Annual Review of Applied Linguistics,* 138–151. Rowley, MA: Newbury House.

———. (1987). Cultural thought patterns revisited. In U. Connor and R. B. Kaplan (Eds.), *Writing across languages: Analysis of L2 text.* Reading, MA: Addison-Wesley.

Leap, W. (1982). Linguistics and written discourse in particular languages: Contrastive studies: English and American Indian languages. In *Annual Review of Applied Linguistics,* 24–37. Rowley, MA: Newbury House.

Lux, P. A. (1991). *Discourse styles of Anglo and Latin American college students.* Unpublished doctoral dissertation, Arizona State University.

Ostler, S. E. (1987). *A study of the contrastive rhetoric of Arabic, English, Japanese and Spanish.* Unpublished doctoral dissertation, University of Southern California.

————. (1987). English in parallels: A comparison of English and Arabic prose. In U. Connor and R. B. Kaplan (Eds.), *Writing across languages: Analysis of L2 text.* Reading, MA: Addison-Wesley.

Purves, A. C. (Ed.). (1988). *Writing across languages and cultures: Issues in contrastive rhetoric.* Newbury Park, CA: Sage Publications.

Smitherman, G. (1986). *Talkin and testifyin: The language of Black America.* Detroit: Wayne State University Press.

Taylor, G., and Chen, T. (1991, September). Linguistic, cultural and subcultural issues in contrastive discourse analysis: Anglo-American and Chinese scientific texts. *Applied Linguistics, 12*(3), 319–336.

Thompson-Panos, K., and Thomas-Ruzic, M. (1983, December). The least you should know about Arabic: Implications for the ESL writing instructor. *TESOL Quarterly, 17*(4), 609–623.

Tsao, F. F. (1982). Linguistics and written discourse in particular languages: Contrastive studies: English and Chinese (Mandarin). In *Annual Review of Applied Linguistics,* 99–117. Rowley, MA: Newbury House.

Whorf, B. L. (1956). *Language, thought and reality.* Cambridge, MA: MIT Press.

Effects of Culture on Writing

Dunlap, L. (1990). Language and power: Teaching writing to third world graduate students in U.S. planning schools. In B. Sanyal (Ed.), *Breaking the boundaries: A one-world approach to planning education.* New York: Plenum Press.

Fox, T. (1990). Basic writing as cultural conflict. *Journal of Education, 172*(1), 65–83.

Freire, P. [1973] (1981). *Education as the practice of freedom.* New York: Continuum.

Lu, M. Z. (1987, April). From silence to words: Writing as struggle. *College English, 49*(4), 437–448.

Matalane, C. (1985, December). Contrastive rhetoric: An American writing teacher in China. *College English, 47*(8), 789–808.

Ngugi wa Thiong'o. (1986). *Decolonizing the mind: The politics of language in African literature.* Portsmouth, NH: Heinemann.

Orwell, G. (1950). Politics and the English language. In *Shooting an elephant and other essays.* London: Secker and Warburg.

Pharis, K. E. (1987). *A study of faculty perceptions of foreign graduate student writing.* Unpublished doctoral dissertation, University of Illinois at Urbana-Champaign.

Purves, A. C., and Purves, W. C. (1986, May). Viewpoints: Cultures, text models, and the activity of writing. *Research in the Teaching of English, 20*(2), 174–197.

Ray, R. (1987). *Academic literacy and non-native writers.* Unpublished doctoral dissertation, University of Michigan.

Shen, F. (1989, December). The classroom and the wider culture: Identity as a key to learning English composition. Staffroom Interchange. *College Composition and Communication, 40*(4), 459–466.

Understanding Classroom Racism

Balenger, V. J., Hoffman, M. A., and Sedlacek, W. E. (1992, May). Racial attitudes among incoming white students: A study of 10-year trends. *Journal of College Student Development, 33,* 245–252.

Blanchard, F. (1992, May 13). Combating intentional bigotry and inadvertently racist acts. *The Chronicle of Higher Education,* 1.

Harvard Educational Review. (1990). *Facing racism in education.* Preprint Series No. 21.

McIntosh, P. (1989, July/August). White privilege: Unpacking the invisible knapsack. *Peace and Freedom,* 10–12.

Perlmutter, P. (1992). *Divided we fall: A history of ethnic, religious, and racial prejudice in America.* Ames: Iowa State University Press.

Steele, C. (1992, April). Race and the schooling of black Americans. *The Atlantic, 269,* 68–78.

Multicultural Teaching

Adams, J. Q., Niss, J. F., and Suarez, C. (1991). *Multicultural education: A rationale for development and implementation.* Macomb: Western Illinois University Foundation.

Border, L. B., and Chism, N. V. M. (Eds.). (1992). *The future is now: A call for action and list of resources.* New Directions for Teaching and Learning, No. 49 (*Teaching for Diversity*). San Francisco: Jossey-Bass.

Garner, B. (1989, Fall). Southeast Asian culture and the classroom culture. *College Teaching, 37*(4), 127–130.

Gill, G. E. (1992, May). The African-American student: At risk. *College Composition and Communication, 43*(2), 225–230.

Harvard Educational Review. (1988, August). *Race, racism and American education: Perspectives of Asian Americans, Blacks, Latinos, and Native Americans.* Special Issue, *58*(3).

Jenkins, M. (1990, Spring). Teaching the new majority: Guidelines for cross-cultural communication between students and faculty. *Feminist Teacher, 5*(1), 8–14.

Nieto, S. (1992). *Affirming diversity: The sociopolitical context of multicultural education.* White Plains, NY: Longman.

Schoem, D., Frankel, L., Zuniga, X., and Lewis, E. A. (Eds.). (1993). *Multicultural teaching in the university.* Westport, CT: Praeger.

Sleeter, C. E., and Grant, C. A. (1987). An analysis of multicultural education in the United States. *Harvard Educational Review, 57*(4), 421–444.

Tatum, B. D. (1992). Talking about race, learning about racism: The application of racial identity development theory in the classroom. *Harvard Educational Review, 62,* 1–24.

Index

Acculturation, resistance to, 72
African American students
  communication style of, 98–100, 102, 137n. 2, 142nn. 14, 19
  examples of writing of, 85–86, 91–92, 94, 100–101, 103–106
  indirectness in writing of, 99
  resistance to mainstream style by, 85–86, 91–92, 94–97
  teaching strategies with, 102–103
African traditional wisdom, 49–50
Analytical writing, definition of, 125–126
Analytical writing, problems with. *See also* Collectivist writing style; Contextual emphasis; Indirect writing style; Strategies for teaching; Transitions, problems with
  ancient wisdom orientation in, 57–58, 61–62, 63–64
  digression, 8–9, 13–14, 117–118
  Fox's research methods, xiii–xix
  Fox's research results summarized, xix–xxi
  language-related problems, 78–79, 80–81, 112, 132–133, 136, 140n. 4
  mainstream vs. world majority problems, xiv, 14–15, 26–27, 54, 74
  overgeneralization, 9, 29–30
  summarized, xiii–xvi, 1
  teachers' perceptions of, xiv–xv, 1–2, 61, 69–70, 136
  theme problems, 15–16, 18, 27
  thesis problems, 1, 53–54, 116–117
Ancient wisdom systems
  created wisdom systems compared to, 47–51
  creativity within, 60–61
  cross-cultural similarities in, 139n. 2
  education within, 51–53, 56, 60–61, 62
  educational adaptations to western knowledge systems, 50–51
  opinions and, 56–57
  quotation use and, 61–62
  thesis problems and, 53–54, 116–117
  transition problems and, 53, 58

  Western research on, 58–61
  writing styles and, 57–58, 61–62, 63–64
Angolan student writing, 29–31
Argentinian student writing, 8–9
Athabaskan culture, 21, 138–139n. 3
Audience
  collectivist writing style and, 41
  indirect writing style and, 22
  problems with choice of, 131–132, 136
Authority. *See also* Ancient wisdom systems; Quotations, use of
  anthropological research on, 139–140n. 4
  mainstream student approach to, 54–55, 62–63
  world majority student approach to, 53–54, 56, 61–62, 134

Background information. *See* Contextual emphasis
Belenky, M. F., et al., *Women's Ways of Knowing*, 58–59
Brazilian student writing, 21–22
Brazilian traditional education, 53
Burakumin, 87–88, 141nn. 6, 7, 12

Campbell, Bebe Moore, 93, 102
Chilean student writing, 72–74, 77
Chinese American student writing, 9–10, 117–118
Chinese student writing, 63–64
Chinese traditional education, 51–52, 56
Clichés, 45. *See also* Ancient wisdom systems; Originality
Collectivism
  in African American communication style, 99–100
  anthropological research on, 138–139n. 3
  cross-cultural similarities in, 36
  individualist aspects of, 37, 139nn. 4, 5
  in rural Québec, 32–36
  view of individualist societies from, 36

Author

Helen Fox has lived and worked for most of her adult life in various cultures. She taught English as a Second Language to French-speaking adults for ten years in rural Quebec, trained science teachers when she was a Peace Corps volunteer in India, and trained Peace Corps volunteers in nonformal education and community development in West Africa and the South Pacific. She received her master's and doctoral degrees from the Center for International Education at the University of Massachusetts at Amherst, where she directed programs in American culture and language for international graduate students and scholars, trained U.S. business people to work more effectively abroad, and developed and taught graduate-level writing courses for international and U.S. students. She is currently a lecturer at the University of Michigan, where she teaches composition and community development and trains graduate students to teach writing in the disciplines.